THE
LIBRARY TRUSTEE

A Practical Guidebook

BY VIRGINIA G. YOUNG

Editor for the American Library Trustee Association of
the American Library Association

R. R. BOWKER COMPANY

1969, New York & London

Standard Book Number: 8352–0257–7

Library of Congress Catalog Card Number: 74–79430

Printed and Bound in the United States of America

Acknowledgments

MUCH gratitude is due the contributors who have written chapters for this second edition of *The Library Trustee: A Practical Guidebook*. Their gracious readiness to share their knowledge and experience, and the generous use of their talent for writing are deeply appreciated.

Grateful acknowledgment is also expressed to those library trustees, librarians, Friends of the Library, and educators who have made helpful suggestions for this expanded and revised edition.

Five years ago, the first edition of this book was offered to the library trustees with the hope of "helping library trustees understand and measure up to their public trust. . . ." Apparently "the seed fell upon good ground," judging from the alert and intelligent response received from its readership.

To those readers go the appreciative thanks of the editor, together with the renewed hope that this revised edition may prove useful as a handbook of trusteeship.

Foreword

Much is heard today of the sweeping changes which have taken place in the library world. Too often, absorbed in the spectacular spotlight of change, perception fails to take note of what has remained constant in that world: the fine professionalism of the librarians, and the dedicated spirit and inquiring minds of the library trustees.

It is in response to these unchanged intangibles that a second edition of this book has been prepared. As stated in the foreword to the first edition, the purpose of the book is described in its title. With the addition of updated, expanded and new materials, the second edition is again offered as *A Practical Guidebook* to library trustees to help them in the fullest realization of their dedication to building better library service.

Virginia G. Young
Editor

Contents

Chapter One

The Trustee in Today's World

BY DOROTHY S. McALLISTER

AND RUTH WARNCKE

T ODAY OUR society is confronted not only with many new and serious problems, but with great unrest. To fulfill the needs of a rapidly changing world requires the creative use of all of our resources —especially our human and educational resources. Unprecedented opportunities for librarians and trustees are at hand. There are opportunities to see that the library assumes a leadership role in terms of its rich resources for the decision makers of our country. There are opportunities to enlarge the library's educational role for all people, and to expand its services to help the disadvantaged secure the information and knowledge that will enable them to enter the mainstream of American life. Only by fulfilling these opportunities today will the library take its rightful place in the world of tomorrow.

The trustee of today must reconsider the goals and policies of his

---

MRS. McALLISTER is 1969–70 President of the American Library Trustee Association and has served as a member of the Michigan State Board for Libraries.
MISS WARNCKE is the Deputy Executive Director of the American Library Association.

1

library in the light of social and educational changes. These changes affect small communities as well as large. Of special significance to libraries is the fact that our population is characterized by mobility. Many people, including members of minority groups, have come to the metropolitan areas from farms and smaller towns seeking work and other advantages. Others have been transferred by their employers from one locality to another. Still others have moved from the cities to the suburbs, which are spreading so extensively that continuous metropolitan areas are developing in many parts of the United States.

Also significant is the strong movement in this era toward equality of opportunity. Civil rights legislation, especially provisions for equal employment opportunity and training, as well as anti-poverty programs, have made it possible for the disadvantaged and oppressed to see hope for a good life and to take steps to achieve it. Civic disturbances and the violence resulting from misery and frustration place new obligations on public as well as private institutions.

The times are marked by a vast broadening of educational opportunities, and an effort to correct the inequities among suburb, city, and country, and among groups within a city. The provision of higher education for increased numbers of people has made even more serious the plight of those who have not had this opportunity, and also of the basically undereducated. Deepened concern over the large number of illiterates has led to a drive to wipe out illiteracy and to increase the employability of the unskilled and underprivileged.

Much of the impetus for expansion of educational opportunities has come from the growth of technology. Previously learned skills are no longer effective; the effort and time required for many operations have been sharply reduced. Already men and women are finding themselves with many more hours of leisure as well as with the need for retraining as job requirements change and new kinds of work offer new openings for employment. The education of adults has become as essential as the education of children, if adults are to stay productive all their lives and are to continue to learn for self-improvement and development.

Concern has been expressed that the tendency to substitute vocational training for liberal education, and to confuse training and education, may have serious consequences for our society. Equal access to the materials of learning is essential to equip men with the understanding necessary to direct their lives and with the knowledge to participate intelligently as citizens in a democratic government.

Through books and the arts there can be communication among all groups and races; through recourse to history and to the ideas of the past, men are better able to deal with the problems of our time and to plan for the future.

The arts themselves have undergone great changes in this century, changes welcomed by some, and utterly rejected by others. The very standards by which a work is judged are subject to frequent re-evaluation. As the writers, painters, and sculptors achieve greater freedom of expression, attempts at censorship become stronger, and communities are beset by struggles to maintain intellectual freedom.

Decision makers, aware of the many complexities of present day society, must more and more have access to the free flow of information. In this respect, trustees must make very certain that the library is the true leader it must be in providing assistance in solving the many problems that arise.

Of great importance to trustees of public libraries is the fact that, owing to increased recognition by state and federal governments of the vital role of the library in a democracy, money has been made available for library development in amounts beyond anything hitherto envisioned. There is every reason to believe that it will not only continue, but must be increased.

With such governmental interest and support, and with the revolutionary educational and social changes taking place, have come enlarged responsibilities and opportunities for trustees and librarians.

Concept of the Modern Library

The library that meets today's needs reflects, in its practices and in its services, the changes in society. The independent library unrelated to any other is rapidly becoming a thing of the past. Library systems and networks are recognized as essential. The necessity for library service for all of the people can be fulfilled only by developing combinations of libraries that make the most of their pooled resources and use their staff abilities to the greatest advantage. Administrative networks have become more effective through use of electronic communications systems and of other automated devices to increase the speed and efficiency of library operations.

In the modern library, personnel is used in increasingly productive ways. Tasks are described and evaluated and assigned to personnel who are equipped to perform them. The realignment of job assignments not only requires the employment of specialists in such fields as business management and public relations, but frequently makes it possible to employ people of varied backgrounds and sometimes limited formal education, thus opening doors of advancement to them, and supplying needed personnel for routine work in the library. Such employees can be most effective in introducing library service to others of the disadvantaged.

Changes in operation are necessary to provide the services for a modern society. There is a growing awareness of the social role to be played if the library is to do its share in meeting the crisis of new conditions and social upheaval. In order to provide total and equal service for all, the library operation must be based on an understanding of the needs and interests of the people in the area served. Particular attention should be paid to those groups whose needs are so special that conventional library service cannot fulfill them. The undereducated, the functionally illiterate, the non-English speaking, the oppressed minorities, as well as the economically deprived, require specialized services, materials suited to their present and growing capacities, and service outlets that are convenient and welcoming. The poor seldom venture forth from the areas where they live; it is necessary to take the needed services to them, wherever they are.

The aging, and the mentally and physically handicapped, require special facilities ranging from the elimination of stairs to the provision of mechanical page turners and large print books. Finally, in a highly mobile society, every community has its share of families newly arrived and in need of materials and services to equip them to understand their new community and to develop a satisfactory life within it.

Special attention to special groups must take its proportional place in a program of services for the entire population, with particular concern for the adult who has no educational resource other than the public library. The very young people who are out of school, many of whom have already assumed adult responsibilities, need to continue their education, and only the library, by means of a variety of materials, activities, and counseling offers this opportunity.

It is through cooperation with the appropriate private and public agencies, and especially with the schools and other libraries in the area in a carefully planned program, that the public library can serve as a center for culture, information, and recreation for all of the people.

Role of the Trustee

Today the trustee's traditional and continuing responsibility of fulfilling a public trust has new implications: it means maintaining sensitivity to a changing society and taking action to assure the provision of services required of a modern library in meeting the needs of this society. (See Appendix VII.) The new responsibilities of the trustee entail a knowledge of financial aid available from federal and state sources, and of successful projects conducted by other libraries in economic opportunity programs and extension of services to the disadvantaged. They entail the obligation to take full advantage of this financial aid, and to exercise initiative in planning new services.

When the trustee works with staff on planning to meet the changing needs and new demands of the community, he must face stern reality. Properly educated staff must be sought and paid adequately; space must expand with an expanding program; and working conditions must be conducive to health, welfare, and efficiency.

Trustees in large city libraries find themselves at the bargaining table with union representatives of the library staff. Whether the unionization of staff will extend to systems of small library units is open to conjecture, but the trustee in today's world must be aware of good labor relations practices and must be prepared to look at staff demands objectively and in relation to the effective operation of the library and the good of the community.

The traditional role of the trustee has always included interpretation of the library to the community, and of the community to the library. In today's society such a public relations program includes talking with and listening to the less educated as well as the highly educated, the poor as well as the financially secure, the rebellious as well as the stable. In the development of plans and services, the trustees of the modern library need to obtain the suggestions and advice of all segments of the community in order to know their requirements.

As the library's role in the community expands, trustees and librarians have found it of inestimable value to provide information on library needs and problems to lay members of educational, civic, student, and other state organizations, government officials, and leaders in various fields, and to involve them in plans for library development. This has been done successfully in nearly two-thirds of the states by means of a Governor's Conference on Libraries to enlist statewide citizen interest and support. An important aspect of a Governor's Conference is the follow-up by regional and local meetings throughout the state as soon as possible after the Governor's Conference. This follow-up is a responsibility of trustees in each community. It is their opportunity to bring the impact of the Conference to those who could not attend and to inform representatives of local organizations and lay leaders of library needs and services.

Since the board of trustees of a library is in itself a governmental unit, it should develop cooperative relationships with the officers of government. As modern governments become more complex, the task of maintaining communication becomes more difficult. The trustee must be a close observer of the political process and a firm spokesman concerning the responsibilities of government for the provision of library service. A united approach to social and educational problems is developing in many communities; it is necessary for trustees to become more involved in this effort and to see that libraries contribute to it in every possible way.

Are Library Boards Necessary?

From time to time the role of the library board is questioned. It is argued that the affairs of the library have become too complex and technical to be dealt with by laymen. City managers or other professionally trained officials often prefer to deal directly with the librarian without the intervention of a policy making group. Some librarians fail to see the value of a board of trustees. In some communities library boards have been abolished to be replaced by citizens' advisory committtes with no legal power.

Accepted general practice, however, by public as well as by private institutions of a public nature, is to separate policy making from administration as the best way to assure the efficiency and effectiveness of an institution. Moreover, the librarian's time and energies are always used to capacity by administrative and other duties. He needs the assistance of representative lay people in keeping him informed of changing community needs, in maintaining contact with, and interpreting library services to the public, and in obtaining adequate funds. The community, in turn, needs the trustees as its voice in the control and operation of one of its educational institutions. And finally, government officials need contact with a lay group charged with seeing that the government's intent to provide effective library service is carried out. Where library boards are ineffective, it is not because they are not needed; rather, the reasons may be that qualified persons are not selected; that the board is not educated as to its responsibilities and duties; or that once in office, the trustees do not give the library sufficient time and attention.

Many librarians find that a capable, alert, and active board of trustees is a source of wise counsel and valuable support, responsive to professional leadership. Two prevalent and pressing needs are for higher staff salaries and for many more librarians. It is more appropriate and effective for the trustees than for the librarian to seek an increase in the librarian's salary; indeed, it is embarrassing for the librarian to do so. And the trustees, through contact with the public and with guidance counselors, can promote recruitment for librarianship among all groups.

The continuance of the trustee function is largely dependent on sound state and local laws defining the duties and responsibilities of trustees and determining the establishment and maintenance of libraries and on the qualifications of those selected for the governing board. But each trustee in the long run is responsible for his own education and performance. He must keep up to date on library developments, participate in state and national library trustee organizations, and study thoroughly the need and potentials of the library he serves. He must be committed to excellence in library service and be tireless and fearless in taking whatever action is necessary to achieve it.

Chapter Two

Duties and Responsibilities of Trustees

BY VIRGINIA G. YOUNG

Today's library trustee has undertaken responsibility for a changing and complex institution. There is a vast difference between a modern library with its many services and the mausoleum for books which prevailed many years ago. As great a difference has taken place in the implications of trusteeship. Any archaic misconception of the library trustee should be classed with the outdated cryptlike gloom of yesterday's library. These unrealistic images, together with the stock caricature labeled "librarian" (she of the repressive glare and the finger on lip), should be firmly retired from cliché to oblivion.

Responsibility for control of the library, vested in the library board, makes heavy demands upon the time and thought of the library trustee. Services undreamed of a few years ago are now part of every library's program. Modern educational methods, new technical aids, the general and specialized needs of the public, all require versatility and know-how in the board members charged with the responsibility for the library.

MRS. YOUNG is a member of the board of the American Library in Paris, Past President of the Missouri State Library Commission, and Past President of the American Library Trustee Association.

Purpose of the Library Board

Trusteeship by definition is the agency of a person or persons designated to act as governors or protectors over property belonging to another. Since a public library belongs to its entire community, library boards have been created by law to act as citizen control or governing body of the library. Library trustees accordingly are public officials and servants of the public, and the powers delegated to library boards are a public trust.

Duties and responsibilities inherent in this public trust may be loosely classified as being of two kinds: the legal responsibilities specifically enjoined upon the board by statute, and the practical responsibilities dealing with day-to-day operation of the library.

The statutory board powers, such as fiduciary responsibility, handling of buildings and real estate belonging to the library, and control of the library's finances, are clearly defined in the state and municipal laws affecting libraries. These legal responsibilities are discussed in detail in other chapters, in relation both to law and to finances. One word of reminder here: statutory responsibilities of a library board are binding. Trustees at all times must accept and abide by this fact.

Duties of Board and Librarian Are Different

The board's multiple responsibilities covering the actual operation of the library bear directly upon every aspect of its program. This has often led to the mistaken belief that the board's duties and responsibilities overlap those of the librarian, a misconception which can lead to endless confusion and misunderstanding.

It cannot be too firmly emphasized that the library board represents overall citizen control of the library, whereas the librarian's training and experience have been in administration of the library. A clear-cut definition of the duties of each is shown in the following chart.

Although duties of the librarian and the library board fall into roughly parallel areas, the obligations and responsibilities of each are entirely separate. Properly comprehended and performed, these parallel duties will strengthen and complement each other, without risk of competitive or divided authority.

Duties and Responsibilities[1]

OF THE LIBRARY BOARD

1. Employ a competent and qualified librarian

2. Determine and adopt written policies to govern the operation and program of the library

3. Determine the purposes of the library and secure adequate funds to carry on the library's program

4. Know the program and needs of the library in relation to the community; keep abreast of standards and library trends; plan and carry out the library program

5. Establish, support, and participate in a planned public relations program

6. Assist in the preparation of the annual budget

7. Know local and state laws; actively support library legislation in the state and nation

8. Establish among the library policies those dealing with book and material selection

9. Attend all board meetings and see that accurate records are kept on file at the library

10. Attend regional, state, and national trustee meetings and workshops, and affiliate with the appropriate professional organizations

11. Be aware of the services of the state library

12. Report regularly to the governing officials and the general public

OF THE LIBRARIAN

1. Act as technical advisor to the board; recommend needed policies for board action; recommend employment of all personnel and supervise their work

2. Carry out the policies of the library as adopted by the board

3. Suggest and carry out plans for extending the library's services

4. Prepare regular reports embodying the library's current progress and future needs; cooperate with the board to plan and carry out the library program

5. Maintain an active program of public relations

6. Prepare an annual budget for the library in consultation with the board and give a current report of expenditures against the budget at each meeting

7. Know local and state laws; actively support library legislation in the state and nation

8. Select and order all books and other library materials

9. Attend all board meetings other than those in which his own salary or tenure are under discussion; may serve as secretary of the board

10. Affiliate with the state and national professional organizations and attend professional meetings and workshops

11. Make use of the services and consultants of the state library

12. Report regularly to the library board, to the officials of local government, and to the general public

[1] Virginia G. Young, *The Trustee of a Small Public Library*. Number 3 of the series: The Small Public Library. Chicago. American Library Association, 1962. Reprinted with permission.

The Board's Duties Discussed

Although the twelve specific duties of the library board shown in the foregoing chart are not necessarily listed in the order of their importance, the first and second named are literally paramount. Employment of a librarian and making of the library's policy are two functions of the board which must be carried out before a workable program for the library can be formulated. These, together with most of the other responsibilities listed, merit chapters of their own, and are discussed at length elsewhere in this book.

The Board's Role in the Community

The duty listed as to "know the program and needs of the library in relation to the community; keep abreast of standards and library trends; plan and carry out the library program," covers not only the trustee's obligation to know the library, but to interpret the library to the community. This liaison role, as interpreter between library and community, is an important part of the public trust assumed by service on a library board.

As layman and as community representative on the library's governing board, it devolves upon the trustee to bring the public's point of view and the community's needs into plans for the library's program. As a public official charged with control of the library, it is also part of the trustee's liaison work to make the community aware of the library's need for financial and moral support, and of the plans and programs for development of better library service. Effective library service is that which meets, so far as possible, the needs of the total community, placing the library in its proper relationship of service in the community picture. Only the library trustee is in the unique position of forming a link between the public and the professional library world, through first-hand knowledge and experience in both areas.

The Trustee's Obligation to Know

Obviously this important liaison work, so necessary to building a favorable climate for the library's progress, cannot be carried out unless the library board knows its library. Indeed, the alert trustee should realize the need for knowing libraries as a whole—other public libraries, school libraries, college and university libraries. What are the problems of libraries? How are the problems being met? What is the basic philosophy of good library service? How does the trustee's own library fit into the overall library picture? What is the library profession as a whole thinking and talking about? What are the comparative values of new trends in library techniques, and how do they fit into the needs of the community for total library service?

The Board's Duty to Plan

The trustee's duties include the obligation to plan for the library's future growth and development—to think creatively. Channels for learning about the library are plentiful. Study of the library literature, observant visits to other libraries, consultation with the librarian, advice from the state library, all offer education to the trustee who honestly desires to learn.

Every trustee who enters upon service to the library has a choice to make: to be indifferent, acquiescent and ineffectual, or to learn everything possible about the responsibilities of trusteeship and so fulfill the public trust.

An Obligation to the Library Profession

Another unwritten—and indeed, frequently unknown—obligation of the library board is responsibility toward recruitment for the library profession. In general, until a library board begins to search for a qualified librarian to employ, the alarming shortage of trained librarians is not realized. There are today many more vacant positions existing than there are trained persons to fill them. Libraries are expanding and growing, new and specialized positions are being created, and the need for librarians is acute.

To meet the need, new candidates for the profession must be enlisted, and here the library trustee can again form an important link between the professional library world and the public. Contacts with faculty advisers at high school and college level and with students themselves, speeches before civic groups, and use of the library's public relations program can present the advantages of professional librarianship as a career. Young persons whose present employment in the business world does not offer the interests and benefits that a library career would confer may be informed about the library profession. Staff members of the library may need encouragement to advance toward professional standing.

Letters from the library board to the board of education could point out the importance of encouraging topnotch teachers and students in the school system to attend library school, with the particular aim of supplying the need for school librarians. Women's organizations should be contacted about librarianship as a challenging profession for their members, especially as a "second career" for the women whose families are grown, and who wish to use their education and talents in worthwhile service to the community. State and local planning and development bodies should be made aware of the value of including the best possible library service in their goals for community planning.

The Public Trust

The ultimate purpose of a library program must be to render adequate service to its community and to the individuals in it. These individuals form the public which in turn looks to the library board as its deputies to carry out a library program which satisfactorily provides this important community service.

Responsibilities of library board members are both tangible and intangible. Some are of immediate and practical effect; others have a far-reaching influence on the library's future.

The dedicated trustee accepts them all as part of faithfully rendered service to the library. These responsibilities constitute the board member's public trust.

Chapter Three

Qualifications and Appointment of Trustees

BY VIRGINIA G. YOUNG

Good library trustees are neither born nor made; they create themselves through inner growth of education and experience in trusteeship, built upon personal background and attributes. Individual backgrounds and characteristics may vary, but good library trustees have certain qualifications in common.

Desirable Qualifications for a Trustee

Surveys of the library literature and lists compiled by trustee organizations agree on the following qualifications for effective trusteeship:

1. Interest in the library, in the community, and in the library's relationship to the community
2. Readiness to devote time and effort to carrying out the duties of trusteeship
3. Recognition of the library's importance as a center of information, of community culture, recreation, and continuing education
4. Close acquaintance with community social and economic conditions, and with groups within the community
5. Ability to work well with others: board members, librarian and staff members, and the public served by the library

6. An open mind, intellectual curiosity, and respect for the opinions of others
7. Initiative and ability to establish policies for successful operation of the library and impartial service to all its patrons
8. Courage to plan creatively, to carry out plans effectively, and to withstand pressures and prejudices
9. Devotion to the library, its welfare and progress

To this list of attributes held in common by all good trustees, every individual board member brings personal experiences and skills which may serve the library well. Professional experience in law, architecture, education, and accounting, for example, can be very valuable to a board member. Practical business experience, executive ability, management skills, and plain common sense are useful contributions. Often the library board has cause to be grateful to board members with political know-how.

The qualities listed are of nearly equal importance, although one has frequently been overlooked as essential. No library trustee can give full measure of service without willingness to give time and effort to the duties of trusteeship. The most brilliantly endowed trustee who does not attend board meetings will not render as much real service to the library as one less gifted who is faithful and diligent in performance.

Devotion to the library's welfare and progress is perhaps the most important single qualification, for all the others stem from it. It would be better for the trustee who lacks this devotion not to be on the board at all, for as Barrie's Maggie Shand said of charm, "If you don't have it, it doesn't much matter what else you have."

The Board Should Represent Total Community

For many years, whether by accident or design, library boards were invariably drawn from groups of similar background and experience. Today's library has a new and increasing importance to the total community, and a well-balanced board should represent a cross section of the community.

The outmoded notion that trustee appointments should be made only in a small class of "cultured" persons is disproved today by the very real interest in libraries evidenced by business, industry, and labor. Every segment of today's society has a stake in the community library, and the needs and desires of every segment of society should be represented in the library's program. The resulting broad diversity of viewpoints will be not only democratic, but conducive to a healthy and living relationship between library and community.

Appointment or Election of Trustees

Library trustees usually serve by appointment, although in several states trustees are elected by the voters and must campaign for the office and take their chances at the polls as do other elective officials.

Trustees serve without compensation under appointment from the public official or governing body in charge of the political division in which the library is located. Governors, county judges, mayors, city managers, city councils, and boards of commissioners are all appointing bodies for their various library boards. Terms of office may vary in different localities.

Unless the appointing official is aware of the importance of choosing a trustee of desirable qualifications, it is only natural that such appointments may often be left to chance or political patronage. It is only fair to state here, however, that in many cases trustees who have come onto library boards in this manner have felt the influence and appeal of the library to such an extent that they have proved to be excellent trustees. These trustees may or may not be the exceptions, but certainly the welfare of the library is too important for service on its board to be considered merely in the light of a status symbol.

The solution has frequently been to communicate with the appointing official, setting out qualifications necessary for a good library trustee, and stressing the importance of such appointments. This communication may well be carried through by the state trustee organization, although it is entirely ethical for a library board to lay these facts before their own appointing officials. When a vacancy occurs, the communication may be accompanied by a list suggesting names of individuals who would be valuable library trustees. The list of desirable qualifications is comprehensive enough to allow appointing officials wide latitude of choice.

When library trustees are elected, it is incumbent upon the local library board to encourage good and qualified candidates to run for the office. Since the board members are themselves elected public officials, it is perhaps best that the board take no official part in the campaign. Individual board members are of course free to back a candidate of their choice by aiding in his campaign and helping to get the vote out on election day.

Tenure of Service

Even in cases where the trustee's term is defined by law, tenure of service may be drawn out to indefinite length by reappointment. Where trustees are elected, a trustee deeply interested in the library may run for the office again and again. So frequently has this been done and so lengthy has the tenure become in such cases, that a natural question arises: would it be better to have someone else serve who might bring new ideas and varied viewpoints?

Continuity of service, it may be argued, makes up in valuable experience and education in trusteeship what may be lost by absence of new blood on the board. The trustee who has devoted time and effort to learning as much as possible about the duties and responsibilities of board membership is without doubt valuable to the library. But it may be argued on the other hand that when the service of even a valuable trustee is terminated, the library still has a staunch, well-informed friend in the former trustee, and has at the same time the advantage of new faces and fresh thinking on the board.

Certainly a self-perpetuating board is much like closed-circuit television: the image reaches only the favored few. Having the best interests of the library at heart, the good library trustee would rather step down than see the library program stagnate. This question of voluntary termination by resignation or refusal of reappointment or re-election is one which requires honest self-appraisal. Perhaps the criterion by which to decide is simply to assess one's value to the library now, and to weigh that value against the benefits to be derived from thoughts and energies of new board members.

One workable solution to the dilemma has been found in staggered board terms, so that at all times senior board members are balanced by newcomers in trusteeship. Another solution has been statutory prohibition of self-succession, allowing for a certain period of time to elapse before a trustee is reappointed or re-elected.

In the final analysis, the problem is best solved by the trustee's own attitude. A sincere devotion to the progress and welfare of the library means giving to it lifelong service, whether on or off the board.

Chapter Four

Organization of the Library Board

BY MINNIE-LOU LYNCH

Every board of directors' meeting has three essentials: a quorum of its members, a well-prepared agenda, and an alert and informed chairman presiding. Effective library board meetings need more: every board member should attend, if the community's image is to be faithfully reflected in the board's actions. The well-balanced board being a cross section of the community, it should be taken for granted that each member will be in his place at meetings. Willingness to attend board meetings is a primary responsibility of trusteeship. There are no proxies in fulfilling the public's trust.

Provision for regularly scheduled meetings of the board should be written into the bylaws, and minutes of each meeting should be kept. These written records constitute a history of the library and of the board's actions, invaluable for future reference and consultation.

Individual library boards should settle upon dates, times, and frequency of meetings. The bylaws should cover these points, as well as establishment of a quorum, procedure on special or called meetings of the board, appointment of special committees, and amendments to the bylaws.

MRS. LYNCH is Chairman of the Allen Parish (La.) Library Board of Control, and Past President of the American Library Trustee Association.

Some boards appoint the librarian as secretary of the board meetings. This procedure has two advantages: it enables the librarian to maintain close rapport with the board's thinking, and it gives the board members the benefits of conferring with the librarian.

Preparing the Agenda

The librarian should prepare the agenda in close consultation with the board chairman. Copies of the agenda should be sent out in advance to every board member so that none will attend the meeting unprepared.

In preparing the agenda, one chief aim should be kept always in mind: to make every board meeting meaningful. More absenteeism results from simple boredom than from any other cause. Routine business there always must be, but the community leaders who serve as members of the library board will come to feel repeated routine meetings a waste of their time, falling far short of their purpose in undertaking trusteeship of the library. The library board that must resort to frantic last-minute calls to turn out a quorum is a library board in trouble, and the apathy of the "bored" members will be reflected by a stagnating library program.

There is plenty of latitude allowed by the category of "new business" to offset this threat. Library boards are the planning officials of the library, and time should be reserved at every board meeting for consideration of the library's next progressive step. Creative thinking by the board may be sparked in any number of ways: by reports from trustees or special committees assigned to explore new trends, by informed professional advice and suggestions from the librarian, by reports on regional and national conferences, and visits to other libraries. Here is an ideal spot for board members to benefit from talks by professional consultants from the state library or elsewhere. Whatever broadens the horizons of the board and stimulates creative thinking for the library's progress should be provided for and included to some degree in the agenda for every board meeting.

The Order of Business

Consultation of the literature and of handbooks of many state trustee associations reveals the following order of business as approved by the majority of library boards:

Roll call
Reading of minutes of previous meeting
Correspondence and communications
Report of librarian
Financial report and approval of expenditures
Report of standing committees
Report of special committees
Unfinished business
New business
Adjournment

Routine business should be disposed of as quickly as possible to leave time for discussion of other matters. The board's long-range plans should always be kept as a "live" subject for such discussions, and never shelved or taken for granted. The board's continuing study of the standards and ways of achieving them should also be kept before the members.

Some library boards move the librarian's report out of the "routine business" category into the area of stimulating discussion by using this report as a basis for evaluating the work of the librarian and the progress being made on the library's overall program. Both board and librarian can gain much in this manner, as accomplishments, obstacles, and plans are reviewed.

The Role of the Chairman

Leadership and tact are called for in almost equal degrees in the chairman of a library board. A thorough knowledge of the library's programs and problems is needed for intelligent conduct of board meetings. Cordial cooperation with the librarian and with other board members smooths the way for efficient operation of the library's business.

Almost every group contains one voice which is heard more often and more loudly than the others. Sometimes this articulate voice denotes superior leadership and information; sometimes not. It is part of the chairman's responsibility to discern this tendency and tactfully hold it in check, making sure that every board member has a chance to be heard. It is entirely possible that the most valuable contributions will come from some less vocal member. If all are democratically given a voice and a vote, the board will avoid the risk of being a mirror for the opinions of any one member.

Orientation of New Members

As soon as a new trustee is appointed, the chairman and the librarian should give the new board member a helpful welcome by following the Trustee Orientation Program as developed by the American Library Trustee Association (See Appendix I). This program may be used either at a full board meeting, or informally in the librarian's office, with the chairman, the librarian, and the new trustee forming a question-and-answer trio. The more informal group is recommended for a relaxed and personal atmosphere, but at least one orientation should be given before the board for its inspirational effect.

The orientation program summarizes the meaning of trusteeship, grounds the new board member in information about the library, introduces him to staff members, and to the organization and administration of the library, and arms him with general information about the responsibilities of trusteeship at state and national, as well as local levels. The librarian should supplement the program with materials drawn from the recommended reading list, for the new member's self-education.

At the new trustee's first board meeting, a wise chairman will immediately give him an assignment, enabling the novice to identify himself with the library's program and the board's functions from the very outset of his service.

Standing and Special Committees

Some library boards, usually those of larger libraries, maintain standing committees of three or more board members who are assigned to follow various phases of the library's operation and program and report to the board with recommendations.

However, there is a decided trend to have the board work as a committee of the whole in general areas of library operation, programs, and expansion. This method involves each member in every phase of the library's development and avoids creating "specialists" artificially.

Special committees may be created from time to time to carry out limited projects on which the total board cannot spend its time. These committees may be empowered to seek advice from members of the community and to do research as background for a decision by the whole board.

Individual library boards will find useful ways in which to involve all members, preferably in the total library picture.

Controversies, Private and Public

Disagreements, differences of opinion, and personality clashes are bound to occur from time to time in any group. Library boards should be democratically administered, with every member having the right to express an opinion and vote accordingly. A sagacious chairman will encourage discussion while not allowing matters to get out of hand, and persons qualified to serve on a library board should include among those qualifications an adult acceptance of the will of the majority.

Esprit de corps should be bigger than any individual feelings, consequently disagreements among board members should not emerge from the board room, to the public detriment of the library. Here is another place where the trustee's devotion to the welfare of the library should ensure the board standing shoulder to shoulder as a solid entity behind its policies, and behind the librarian in carrying out those policies.

The field of library service is in the realm of ideas, and it is but natural that from time to time, citizens or citizen groups who are adherents of ideas opposing the policies of the board will wish to be heard. This is entirely within their rights, and the board's written policies should provide for such contingencies.

Such a request for hearing should be made in writing, and the conditions of the hearing should be made clear in advance to the petitioners, i.e., whether the meeting is to be a closed board meeting or an open public meeting, etc. After the hearing, the board should take such matters under advisement to allow time for its deliberations and action. Once the board has voted its decision, the trustees should again be governed by *esprit de corps* outside the board room. Loyalty to the library's welfare will not encourage either schisms on the board, or feuds within the community.

The Board's Need to Retain an Attorney

Library boards will find it well worthwhile to hire and retain the services of a competent attorney. Every important step in building, property management, contracts, and the framing of favorable library legislation requires legal advice. Should controversial questions arise, particularly in the area of attempted censorship or limitation of the right of freedom to read, the board should be represented by legal counsel.

Sharing Opportunities

Opportunities for responsibility such as chairmanship of the board or of subcommittees should be rotated among board members to avoid domination of the board by a privileged clique. Educational benefits, such as payment of expenses to trustee workshops and conferences, should also be shared democratically among the board members, so that every member has an opportunity to acquire the experience and knowledge of trusteeship to be gained.

Chapter Five

The Trustee
as Policy Maker

BY VIRGINIA G. YOUNG

L IBRARY POLICY has been compared to a road map, and policy, like a map, should be clearly drawn on paper. This written policy should set out the terms of the library's operation: the what, when, where, and how, frequently the who, and sometimes the why.

Policy determines the pulse of a community's library service—availability of library service, terms of staff employment, the objectives of the library's program, and the intellectual freedom which the community has a right to expect. These factors are the structural steel on which a library in its true meaning is raised. Policy is the responsibility of a library board, and except for the employment of a librarian, no other duty of the trustee is more important to the library and its welfare.

What Policy Should Cover

Every library board should determine and record its policies on:

1. General library objectives
2. Hours open; hours of staff duty; holidays
3. Vacation and sick leave for librarian and staff

4. Salary schedule; personnel classification chart; retirement provisions
5. Type and quality of books and other library materials to be added to the library collection
6. Charges for lost books; fines on overdue books
7. Services to schools; to specialized groups
8. Special services: to nonresident borrowers, use of meeting hall, etc.
9. Cooperation with other libraries
10. Acceptance of gifts and memorials
11. Methods of extending services: branch libraries, bookmobiles, participation in library system, etc.
12. Public relations and publicity
13. Payment of expenses for trustees and staff to attend library conferences, workshops, and professional meetings
14. Payment of state and national association dues for board members and for the library

Flexibility Where Needed

Policy should be clearly stated, giving a firm foundation for the librarian's administration of the library and the relationships of the staff with the public. Except where details are essential, as in hours of operation, salary schedules, and the like, library policy should be expressed in broad terms, since it is a basis for procedure and need not include details of procedure. It goes without saying that policy must rest upon the legal basis of laws applicable to the operation of libraries.

Library board members should carefully consider each item of policy before it is adopted and recorded. Often the librarian is a source of informed recommendation for new or changed policy, growing out of day-to-day administration of policy and constant contact with the public. Once adopted, a policy should have the support of the entire board, the librarian, and the staff, and it is the board's moral obligation to stand behind the librarian in carrying out policies. Boards are most frequently called upon to support policies in the field of public relations and of book selection.

Firmness of policy and its administration should not denote rigidity, and the library board should keep an open mind toward needed changes and revisions of policy. Frequently new needs supersede previous ones; often a community's whole picture can change in a short space of years. The library board should be prepared to move with the times, and to revise or change its policies accordingly. Provision for an annual review of policies should be made to keep them current.

Policy on Operation

Library boards should make every effort to have the library open as long as possible, and the *ALA Standards* governing the accepted minimum hours of operation per week should be complied with if at all possible. The library standing closed and locked is a dead library so far as the community is concerned.

Hours of staff duty, salary schedules, and leave and retirement provisions should be as generously framed and administered as the library's financial resources will permit. A library board, like every other employer, will get exactly what it pays for, and cut-rate salaries offer no inducement to good librarians and staff members. Consultant service from the state library, reference to the library periodicals, and comparison with similar libraries are the best guides for a library board in determination of salary schedules and working conditions for the librarian and staff.

Book Selection Policies

Once a fairly routine item in the library's policy, book selection has come to be a vital area in today's world of controversial ideas and approaches. Library board members must make an honest appraisal of the question of intellectual freedom before framing their policies in this field. Once the policy is adopted, it should be adhered to fairly and impartially.

As administrator of the board's policies, the librarian is sometimes caught up in the crosscurrents of opposing ideas. Here again, devotion to the library and its welfare should weld the board into solid backing for the librarian and defense of intellectual freedom for the community.

The ALA Committee on Intellectual Freedom serves as an advisory body to the Association, to the profession, and to trustees faced with the problem of censorship and interference with intellectual freedom in the library.

Library boards should also be familiar with the provisions of the "Library Bill of Rights," adopted by the Council of the American Library Association to meet new demands, and with the "Freedom to Read Statement" endorsed by the Council of ALA. These statements constitute strong backing from the American Library Association, offering encouragement to the library board faced with controversy and litigation.

Whether such controversy arises from the ill-informed, the malcontent, or from honest opposition of ideas, the library board must stand firm and unified behind the principle of intellectual freedom, and behind its librarian in carrying out that principle.

Special Services: Schools

Another item once routine, but currently acute, is service to students. The population explosion, overflowing school enrollments, and new impetus for education has turned numbers of students into the public libraries of the nation. The limited scope of the school libraries has proved unable to contain the swelling demands of the thronging students, who then turn to the public library for reference material and study space. In turn, adult patrons are almost crowded out of the community library and at times are deprived of books and services preempted by the students.

Obviously, the problem cannot be solved overnight, and pending the solution, libraries must continue to make every effort to meet the legitimate demands of students and of adult patrons as well. Present resources should be re-evaluated and used to their fullest potential. Only by understanding and cooperation among all types of libraries can the problem be met.

The first essential is close and frank consultation between the librarian and the public school librarians as to what is needed and what is available in the way of services to students. The public librarian will offer the fullest possible cooperation, always with the reservation that the library's services are not subject to takeover by students or any other special group with resulting limitation of services to the general public. It should be further pointed out that it must be the library's policy to build a collection to meet the general needs of the community, and that a disproportionate share of the book purchases cannot be devoted to student needs any more than to the needs of any other special group.

Much the same situation exists between public librarians and college librarians in communities where college students add their requirements to a situation already complicated between students of the elementary and secondary schools and the demands of the general public.

Once the librarians come to a candid and mutual understanding of what can and cannot be made possible, the public librarian is in a position to make informed recommendations to the library board, and policy can be worked out accordingly.

Title III of the Library Services and Construction Act is concerned with Interlibrary Cooperation of all types. The local public library can participate in this program with the state library in helping to solve some of these problems.

Special Services: Groups

Special services offered by libraries provide an excellent channel for public relations, and for building up warm and friendly support for the library within the community. Civic clubs, study clubs, Great Books groups, garden clubs, and business firms and associations have found the local library a rewarding host. In cooperation with the librarian, additions to the library's collection covering the special interests of such groups are often made, and their gratitude is usually expressed in practical gifts and appreciative support for the library.

Most specialized groups are keenly interested in knowing what the library offers in their particular fields, in suggesting additions to the collection, and often in donations of books and related materials. The library board should be alert to the needs of these groups in making long-range plans for the library's program. Too often libraries operate on the basis of what is available to these groups, whereas every effort should be made to ascertain their needs and provide for them.

Use of the library's meeting hall or board room by these groups is part of the library's community relationship. At times when the library needs support in an election, in the legislature, or before the governing body, services to these groups usually prove to have been bread cast upon the waters, and the members repay the library handsomely by backing the library's plans and programs.

The Friends of the Library are a unique group within the community, in that they are organized for the purpose of themselves serving the library. Friends of the Library are discussed at more length in a separate chapter, but they must be included among any groups listed as special. The library board and librarian who work cooperatively with the Friends of the Library will have cause for gratitude.

Special Services: The Handicapped

Services to the blind and otherwise handicapped of the community should be a part of every library program to the fullest measure possible. These are the citizens whose need of the library resources is perhaps greater than any others. Provision to meet those needs should be in every library budget to some degree.

Not every library can afford a collection of Braille or Talking Books, or the services of a trained specialist in this field. Of course, the Library of Congress does provide both books in Braille and Talking Books to various centrally located libraries as regional centers throughout the United States. These materials may be obtained from the regional centers. Librarians and trustees should be familiar with the center nearest them in order to be on their mailing list so this service can be given. But every library, no matter how small or poorly financed, can afford to take certain practical steps toward serving these patrons. Any library can manage to do some or all of the following:

1. Consult with the state library and the headquarters of the American Library Association as to free materials available.
2. Send the librarian or a designated staff member to workshops or conferences on the subject.
3. Build a collection of records and tapes for loan to the blind and the shut-in.
4. Build a collection of visual aids for loan to the deaf.
5. Arrange pick-up and delivery service of books, records, and materials to shut-ins.
6. Arrange at least one street-level entrance to the library to accommodate wheel chairs and crutches.

Delivery service to shut-ins should include service to the community's hospitals. If the library's site and location preclude a street-level entrance, the construction of a ramp (also appreciated by heart patients) is always desirable. The library board must consider these patrons and their interests, and provide for them. Government documents are available which may be helpful in this planning.

Title IV, Part B, of the Library Services and Construction Act makes federal funds available to the states to provide library services to the physically handicapped, including the blind.

Special Services: Nonresident Borrowers

Many libraries make a charge for services to nonresident borrowers, feeling this a proper discrimination between the borrower who is not a taxpayer and the regular patrons of the community. Other libraries will not lend directly to nonresidents, insisting that the request must come through the nonresident's own library. This is an indirect and time-consuming method frustrating to the would-be borrower.

The growing trend among libraries today, with increased extension of library support, is for reciprocal lending service to patrons, with the feeling that a responsible borrower who holds a card from his home library should be welcome as such in every other library. The idea of a statewide library card, giving the borrower privileges in every library in his home state, is gaining adherents and a universally accepted library card seems an even more desirable goal.

Individual libraries whose boards have accepted the worth of the idea are pioneering it in their own communities by extending their policies to allow full privileges to nonresident library card holders, and reciprocal agreements with other libraries. Many library systems already have one card for any library in the system and reciprocal borrowing privileges are also being set up between systems.

Charges and Fines Levied

Libraries properly charge for lost and damaged books. Some states have within their library laws a general provision making the keeping of library property a misdemeanor after suitable notification has been given. In that case, board policy is formed within such a framework.

Until recently, most libraries as a matter of routine charged a daily fine for every day a book was kept overdue, usually placing a maximum amount on the total fine, regardless of the length of time the book was kept. This practice can turn into a two-edged sword, however, resulting in complete loss of the book to the library, for many patrons are not aware of the maximum fine charge. The longer the book is overdue, the greater the sum they fear to be penalized. Often the book is accordingly reported as completely lost, stolen, or any knowledge of it at all is disclaimed.

Some libraries are instituting the practice of no charges for overdue books, and report very favorable results in returned books. It has been proven that there are no more books overdue under this system than where fines are charged. Many patrons feel the charging of fines is punitive, and the elimination of this resentment and annoyance opens the way for books to be returned even if somewhat past their due date. Moreover, it has been found in many instances that the staff time consumed in handling fines would be much more valuable used in service to the public than any income derived from fines collected. That most patrons would prefer to return the library books if they could do so without penalty is shown by the enthusiastic response to the annual or semiannual "Forgiveness Day" instituted by some libraries, when patrons are invited to return missing books, "no questions asked."

Policy statements in the area of lost and damaged books and fines levied are best stated in broad terms, which will make possible the widest use of materials and the fewest abuses.

Memorials and Gifts

The practice of memorial gifts to the library has added many fine volumes, record albums, prints, and paintings to library collections. Often the gift is sent with the indication of some special field of interest held by the person to be memorialized, and the book is chosen accordingly. Just as frequently, the librarian is given carte blanche to expend the money as the library needs indicate. These gifts confer lasting benefits and an enduring memorial.

On a larger scale, legacies have provided libraries with gifts ranging from new buildings to reading patios. Even a modest bequest can memorialize the donor to the library's benefit. It is one of the library trustee's responsibilities to present this suggestion to the well-to-do of the community, laying the library needs before testators with delicacy and tact.

Friends of the Library have provided a pattern for donors by consulting with the librarian and the board before embarking on any projected gift or improvement. A prospective donor or legator might be encouraged to similar wisdom and forethought.

Unfortunately, many donors consult only their own wishes, and the library finds itself the unwilling recipient of a legacy earmarked for one specific purpose, or crippled by other restrictions laid down by the testator. Frequently the legacy or gift is in the form of a collection built around some personal interest of the donor, but of little practical general use to the library. If the gift is made free and clear to the library, it may be sold and the proceeds used to acquire necessities, but frequently the gift is hedged with conditions and the title is not clear.

As the royal gift of a white elephant ruined the hapless recipient by upkeep of the princely present, so the gift which a library may not legally dispose of harnesses the library to its maintenance. Unless the library policy on acceptance of gifts clearly gives the librarian a free hand in their disposition, precious space and staff time will go to the unwelcome addition. The small library in need of funds is a particular sufferer in such cases, whereas the proceeds from the sale of a valuable rare book or art object or special collection could have been translated into the practical benefit of new floor covering, additional reference books, or the convenience of an extension telephone.

Accordingly, the board should work out a policy governing acceptance of gifts, which will enable board members and librarian to be tactfully firm as to the conditions permitted.

Extending the Library's Service

Every library dreams of expanding and extending its services both in scope and in population served. As part of the long-range planning, this should be frequently discussed at board meetings, with particular reference to the next step to be taken. Depending upon the size of the library and its financial resources, the manner of extending service may be planned as branch libraries to serve outlying districts of a city, bookmobile service to distant suburbs and adjacent areas, or by participation in a library system. The board's policies governing these channels of extending the library service should be worked out in consultation with the librarian who may call in specialists in the field from the state library, ALA headquarters, and from other libraries.

Certainly the provisions of Title III of LSCA are designed to see that total library resources are available to every individual. Library trustees can take a leadership role in working with the state library to see that this goal is accomplished.

Often when construction of a new central or branch library is proposed, the board will be approached for a hearing on the matter by citizens or citizen groups. The board's policy on hearings of this nature should provide for free discussion and reception of the public's views, with full explanation by the chairman and the librarian of the board's proposed choice of location. The public has every right to pose questions or offer suggestions as to the conduct of this, as well as other business, and the board's policy should be to welcome the public interest in the library and its services.

The Library's Public Relations

Public relations is but another name for the communication between the library and the people it serves. Channels for this communication are many, and like varying wave lengths, may be beamed to reach different groups who make up the general public. It is this communication that creates the community's awareness of the library and acceptance of its program.

So important is a good public relations program in defining the library's place in the community that ample provision should be made in the annual budget to carry on such a program. Furthermore, maintenance of good public relations for the library is part of the obligation of everyone connected with the institution, from the janitor to the chairman of the board.

The most direct contact with and influence upon the public are, of course, carried on by the librarian and staff, and every good librarian instills this understanding in the staff members supervised. But board members, too, have a very particular and very pressing obligation toward the library's public relations, since trustees are tacitly accepted by the public as "image-makers" of the library.

Specifics of the trustee's obligations toward the library's public relations are discussed in another chapter, both for library boards and for individual members. From the standpoint of policy making, an effective and comprehensive program of public relations should be outlined and constantly maintained.

Organization Dues and Meetings

Since it is good management practice for employers to assist employees in maintaining good professional standing, the policy of the library board should be as liberal as finances permit regarding payment of state and national association dues for the librarian. If possible, the board should arrange payment of these dues for other staff members also, as a proper part of in-service training. Expenses to state and national association meetings for the librarian, and for other members of the staff, perhaps in rotation, should be allowed for in making up the budget. These professional meetings are necessary to the growth in librarianship of both head librarian and staff members, and the board owes them every encouragement to participate.

The trustee's need for membership in state and national organizations, and the value of such memberships, are discussed in Chapter Twenty. Too often in the past it has been left to the individual board member to pay such association dues personally, which can work a hardship upon a trustee whose circumstances are not affluent. The unfortunate result has been limitation of self-education in trusteeship by too many board members.

Every library board member should be a member of his state association, and of the American Library Trustee Association, the "trustee division" of the American Library Association. The board's policy in this matter should be to make provision for payment of these dues for the members if financially possible; if not, at least the chairman should be enrolled as a member of both associations and his dues paid.

At least once during his term of office, every library board member should attend an annual conference of the American Library Association, participating particularly in the programs arranged by the American Library Trustee Association. Expenses for the trip should be included in the library budget, and the privilege should be rotated among board members from year to year, giving all a part in the educational benefits of the national meeting.

The entire board should attend the annual meetings and workshops of the state association. Policy of the board should provide for this participation as additional education in trusteeship and in the trends of the library movement.

The Importance of Policy Making

The foregoing sections sketch the broad framework of library policy, giving some idea of its all-inclusive importance to the operation of the library. Devised as it must be to meet immediate needs, policy also necessarily has a far-reaching effect, and this fact should always be kept in mind by the board members as policy is worked out and adopted in various areas.

Policies determined by the library board set the conditions of the library's day-to-day operation and its program through the years, and policy making demands the best in thought and planning from every library trustee.

Chapter Six

Trustee Relationships with Librarian and Staff

BY VIRGINIA G. YOUNG

Human relationships determine the inner climate of the library, and if those relationships are cordial and understanding, the climate will be as warm and pleasant as a June day. Chief among these relationships, because of its effect on the library's overall administration, is that between the library board and the librarian. Policies drawn by the library board delineate the conditions of the library's operation; the librarian chosen by the board carries out these policies. It is for this reason that the board's duties of policy making and employment of a librarian are always shown as of equal and leading importance in any list of trustee responsibilities.

Employment of a Librarian

Since every library board naturally wishes to employ the best talent available to direct the library, care and thought must be taken in filling the post. The first step should be a realistic appraisal of the situation: what particular qualifications are required in the librarian, and what the library can offer the librarian. Consultation with the state library is helpful here, perhaps assisting the board to adjust its requirements or to provide additional inducements to prospective candidates.

Basis for employment once settled upon, the board should consult approved sources of personnel information, such as the state library, professional publications, and accredited library schools. Background and references of applicants should be checked and personal data evaluated by the board before interviews are arranged. Should the board invite a candidate for a personal interview, the board should pay all or part of the applicant's travel expenses.

The final decision requires careful weighing in the balance of personal and professional factors, always with the aim of employing the librarian who will best serve the library program.

Competition is keen for trained and competent librarians, particularly among libraries of comparable size. Smaller libraries often find themselves at a disadvantage against financial inducements offered by larger institutions. This disadvantage can be offset by certain factors which favor the smaller library. Retired librarians with excellent professional backgrounds frequently welcome the challenge of directing a small, progressive library. Or such librarians may prefer a departmental assignment in a large library, where the administrative load is lighter than that of the head librarian. The position and prestige of a librarian in a small town or suburb, and the somewhat less complex living conditions offered, are inviting to trained librarians of all ages.

In employing a librarian, the board has always one primary responsibility: to fill a worthwhile job with a worthy candidate. If this is done, the welfare and progress of the library are assured.

What the Librarian Should Expect of the Board

Once employed, the librarian can properly expect to count on the board's solid support in carrying out the policies of the library's operation. Decisions of the board and changes in policy are not always universally popular. It is the librarian, carrying out these policies in constant direct contact with the public, who is in the line of fire, drawing the criticism of displeased groups or individuals. The board should at all times give unqualified support in defense of the librarian's administration of its policies. In the controversial area of "freedom to read," which today produces so many incidents between library and public, the board should be prepared to stand firm behind its policy on intellectual freedom, and behind the librarian carrying out this policy.

Book selection and purchase is invariably a sensitive area, both between librarian and board, and between library and public. The librarian has a right to expect the board to draw up policy covering this field, stating in broad general terms the type, quality, and standards governing books and other library materials to be added to the library collection. Individual volumes and items selected and purchased within the terms of such policy are the responsibility of the librarian, and a trained, competent librarian expects to conduct book selection and purchase without interference. Any questions or criticisms arising should be discussed between librarian and board at a full board meeting. Any decision made, within the framework of the total library program, by the majority at such a meeting should be unanimously supported by board members regardless of personalities involved.

The librarian has a right to expect a free hand from the board in administering the library operations. As shown by the chart of comparable duties and responsibilities of board and librarian in Chapter Two, it is the librarian's responsibility to interview, recommend, and employ the staff of the library, and to supervise their work. A librarian therefore can properly expect to confer with the board regarding these matters should it become necessary, but to carry out the supervisory and administrative work without interference by the board or any of its members. The chart plainly shows that the two lists of duties and responsibilities are in many ways parallel, but do not overlap, and probably more internal discord springs from overbusy trustees or boards interfering with the librarian's direction of the library and staff than from any other source.

The board is charged with the responsibility of approving the job specifications and salary scale for library staff members. Once these are adopted by the board, the staff positions and their incumbents are supervised by the librarian, and communication between board and staff is properly carried on through the librarian. Should dissatisfaction arise among the personnel, and members of the board are directly approached to intervene, the matter should first be brought to the attention of the librarian. Later it may be necessary for the matter to come up for discussion before a full meeting of the board, with the librarian. Any other action by overzealous board members will undermine the librarian's authority and probably produce the unhappy result of opposing factions and general disorganization within the library.

Protection of the librarian's professional standing and advancement is a clear obligation of the board. In addition to encouragement and financial support for membership in the state and national professional associations, and attendance at meetings, the librarian should be able to count on time to read in order to stay conversant with trends in books and periodicals. It is taken for granted by the community that the librarian will assume a leading place in cultural affairs, but many librarians find themselves so bogged down in housekeeping aspects of library management that the professional standards of librarianship are nearly impossible to maintain. Protection of the librarian's time and opportunity for this important segment of professional advancement should be assured by the board.

Should another post offering professional advancement be tendered the librarian, the board should be entirely willing to cooperate. Often a librarian identifies so completely with a library and a community that he becomes a permanent resident by choice, but every librarian must be free to move on at any time toward improved professional and financial status.

What has been lightheartedly termed "the care and feeding of a librarian" is squarely up to the library board. The librarian necessarily looks to the board to provide an environment of library operation in which creative librarianship can flourish.

What the Board Should Expect

Topnotch professional performance, personal integrity, and a forward-moving library program are sought by every board in appointing a librarian, and every librarian worthy of the name is prepared to meet these expectations.

There is another legitimate claim which the board should make upon the librarian: to be the board's "open door" into the professional library world. Sometimes a library board is not sufficiently alert to its need for education in developments in the library world to make this demand. Sometimes the librarian does not fully recognize this professional obligation to the board members, and consequently does not do enough to introduce trustees to the library's problems, nor keep the board properly informed. Yet such an expectation on the part of the board, fulfilled by the librarian, is an implicit part of any valid relationship between trustees and librarian.

The ways in which the librarian can meet this expectation are various. Every board meeting offers a number of opportunities for such illumination of the members' thinking. Suggestions as to new policy, and the reasoning behind recommendations for changed or amended policy, will inform the board members about the different aspects of the library operation. The period during which the librarian's report is discussed and evaluated at board meetings offers limitless opportunity for exchange of information between librarian and board. The time reserved at board meetings for creative thought and planning, and for discussion of long-range library programs, gives the librarian a chance to broaden the horizons of the library board by reports and suggestions on new and progressive trends in the library world.

The librarian's obligation in this respect also applies to relationships with individual board members who show an interest in learning about their trusteeship. Many highly effective library trustees are frank to give credit for their achievements to the inspiration of a dedicated librarian.

The Two Interpreters

No reciprocal relationship can be built between librarian and board unless at all times it is remembered that each is charged with the responsibility as interpreter to the other: the librarian and board as interpreter of the library world to the layman, the board as interpreter of the community to the librarian. The two interpreter roles are of equal importance. Both viewpoints must be weighed in the balance before the library can take its proper place in the community.

Many a librarian, armed with shining new professional theory, has shattered a lance on the seeming obstinacy and conservatism of the library board. Yet if each recognized the obligation of the other to interpret, a workable understanding could easily be reached. A librarian should be expected to interpret professional trends to the board; the board should be expected to interpret the community picture to the librarian. Each should welcome the other side of the story, as completing the full picture.

The board which persists in considering any innovation proposed by the librarian as a challenge to a duel in the sun is likely to end up standing in its own light. The librarian who persists in proposing an unwelcome innovation simply because it has worked elsewhere should strive for closer rapport with the community. Sometimes all that is needed to bring about a happy ending is a period of preparation and education for the community's final acceptance. This necessity for seeing both sides of the question should bring together the board and the librarian as partners rather than as duelists.

A thoughtful and respectful hearing of one another's point of view is frequently all that is required to bridge the gap and to weld the two interpretations into a common language.

Agreeing to Disagree

Natural differences of opinion arise in every human relationship, and those which occur between library board and librarian can usually be solved by a moderate and understanding approach on both sides. It sometimes happens, however, that differences of opinion go beyond disagreement into dissension, and the working relationship is so severely ruptured that its continuation is not possible.

If the difficulty cannot be resolved by private conference with the librarian, usually undertaken by the chairman at the request of the board, decisive official action must be taken by a full meeting of the board. It is only just to all concerned that the cause of disagreement and resulting board action be clearly stated.

Sometimes it is felt that a librarian has demonstrated deficiencies in filling the post, and that a more adequate replacement should be sought. Again, a private conference communicating the board's decision with courtesy and candor is recommended. Termination of an unsatisfactory connection need not embarrass the librarian's professional future elsewhere.

When dissatisfaction is felt by either side regarding policies, program, or administration of the library, it has been found that impartial consultant service is useful. Analysis of weaknesses and recommendations for strengthening the program can solve an unsettled situation in a constructive fashion. The state library is in a position to counsel and give assistance upon request.

It should be constantly kept in mind that the board's first responsibility is toward the public, to provide adequate and satisfactory library service, and this obligation takes precedence over personalities, prejudices, and partisanship.

The Board's Relationship with the Staff

The library board's relationship with staff members should be exactly that of a corporate board of directors with employees: one of cordial and friendly interest, entirely free from personal intervention between staff member and supervisor. Policy governing job specifications, salaries, and other terms of employment is the responsibility of the board; selection and supervision of personnel are part of the librarian's administrative duties.

It is entirely possible for board members to make provision for the welfare and job advancement opportunities of the library staff without entering into any too-personal friendships or criticisms involving individual employees. Nepotism should also be shunned, and employment of a close relative of any board member should not be considered.

In larger libraries, staff associations are often valuable to promote in-service training, and to give the staff members an impersonal channel through which to communicate requests, suggestions, and complaints to the board. Formation of such a staff association should receive every encouragement from board and librarian.

While employee organizations in the public sector, and particularly in libraries, are not common, they should be recognized. There seems to be an increasing trend in this direction, though no clear-cut patterns have emerged. In the matter of economic considerations, such organizations bargain collectively with the agency or body authorized to make financial commitment on behalf of the governmental unit. The board is involved in negotiating those terms and conditions of employment over which they have discretion and authority to act. For example, such areas usually include a grievance procedure with an impasse provision. Although there may seem to be certain elements of basic opposition of interests in the relationship between management and employees, it can be, in fact, a most cordial and productive relationship.

Furtherance of job advancement interest of staff members is a responsibility of the library board. Fulfillment of the trustee's obligation toward recruitment for the library profession should begin at home, and the library board should make every effort to encourage and assist staff members who wish to make librarianship a career. If the librarian is not fully trained, the board should arrange for leave of absence to cover completion of professional work.

Individually or as a board, trustees can often arrange grants or scholarships leading to complete professional training for employees of the library. If this cannot be done by the board, the possibility of a scholarship program sponsored by the state association and/or state agency should be investigated and supported. This is possible and important to boards of even the smallest libraries.

Scholarship or other financial assistance is often extended to a candidate for librarianship with the provision that the employee return to the library staff for a given period of time. In this way, the library board insures return benefits for the library from the advantages of professional training obtained.

Relationships Sound the Keynote

The working relationships which prevail within the library determine the attitudes of librarian and staff, which in turn determine the quality of the service offered to the public. It is from these attitudes that the public forms its judgments of the library.

There is no field connected with trusteeship which more richly repays the board's thought and effort than the one of human relationships within the library walls. It is the ultimate responsibility of the library board to make sure that an atmosphere of mutual understanding and cordial cooperation exists. Only in this way can the board, the librarian, and the staff unite in a harmonious team effort toward their common goal of better library service.

Chapter Seven

The Trustee
and Planning

BY VIRGINIA G. YOUNG

AND MINNIE-LOU LYNCH

Planning, in this day of ever increasing demands on the library coupled with a growing competition for the scarce tax dollar, has become a most important responsibility of trustees. One of the duties listed in Chapter Two is "know the program and needs of the library in relation to the community; keep abreast of standards and library trends; plan and carry out the library program." Planning has always been the means of recognizing the present situation, of identifying needs, of determining objectives and assigning priorities, and of deciding the action to be taken to achieve the stated goals.

Planning is essentially preparation for change—the look before the leap. Library trustees must never be willing to simply drift from year to year. Practices from the past can be carried forward by sheer inertia. But today's trusteeship calls for creative thinking and positive action.

Someone has said that "it is often easier to act ourselves into a new way of thinking than it is to think ourselves into a new way of acting." Planning means to think ourselves into a new way of acting.

To move the library forward in an age of change necessitates careful planning today. There are some basic assumptions with which trustees will want to begin. (1) Planning is essential. (2) The librarian and board are partners in planning. (3) The end objective of library planning is service to people. (4) Local planning should be related to the overall state plan where one exists.

The planning process in relation to the library requires answers to some basic questions. (1) Where are we? (2) Where do we want to go? (3) How do we get there?

Where Are We?

There are two major ways to determine the answer to the first question: one is to examine the library in relation to the community, and the other is to examine the library in relation to the ALA standards, *Minimum Standards for Public Library Systems*. In the first instance, the board will want to take a good look at the community and its needs. A community survey which will show population patterns and shifts, the general level of education, the kind of employment, the organizational structures present, and other relevant data is invaluable.

There are a number of ways to gather this information. Experts may be brought in. Local groups may be able to furnish parts of the information required. The state library may be able to provide advice and assistance. There is a rich literature on how to survey the community. ALA has provided a notable contribution to this literature in the Library-Community Study with Ruth Warncke as director.

The standards are the yardstick used to measure the library both qualitatively and quantitatively. The board and librarian can discover how the library rates with regard to services such as reference, audio-visual, art collections, institutional, business and industry, adult, young adult, children, disadvantaged, etc. The standards can be used in examining books and other materials, personnel, and physical facilities.

With this evaluation, it is important to keep in mind the necessity of interpretation with reference to the actual community and not to some mythical situation. The data must be good and the interpretation honest .

If the board and librarian have performed well, they should now be able to see in a clear light the community and its needs and whether these needs are being met by present library services and resources.

Where Do We Want To Go?

Here one recognizes a basic difference between "where we are" and "where we want to go" in the matter of the attitude of the decision maker. "Where we are" could be arrived at by any person or team of persons who are skilled in the techniques of gathering information.

But "where we want to go" is something else. This will not only require correct background for evaluation judgment, but will require a commitment to good library service and to its importance in the total community climate. It is this commitment that is the basic responsibility of the trustee as a holder of the public trust.

The library trustee must see the library as the service organization that is basic to all community education and culture, as well as a source of recreation and refreshment.

It is here that planning is clearly related to the goals and objectives of the library. These, of course, should be clearly defined and written down. In order to do this there must be a definite understanding of the overall philosophy of the library and the function that it serves. It should be recognized that goals are simply purposes to be achieved. To express them in terms of short- and long-range plans clarifies the decision maker's intent and assists in the determination of exactly what needs to be accomplished and in what order.

Another important point to remember is that questions asked and judgments made in planning cannot transpire in a vacuum. People who are library users and community interpreters must be involved, i.e., community leaders, city planners, and various related agencies. The ideas and suggestions of these groups must be sought and evaluated.

Before setting down plans, attention should be given also to the overall statewide plan for library development and the place the local library may be expected to fill.

Then the board will want to actually set down long-range and short-term plans, assign priorities, write down what will be involved to achieve the plans, and the steps to be taken in their accomplishment. It is here that the board will have to take a hard look at the budget and at the realistic possibilities for its increase.

Planning often is attempted without serious consideration of the budget, just as budgets sometimes are assembled with little relation to the planning process.

A new approach to budgeting now in use on state levels and in many metropolitan areas is known as PPBS, Planning, Programming, and Budgeting System. PPBS attempts to bridge the gap between planning and budgeting through what has been described as "a systematic approach of coordinated effort."

Boards seeking to become knowledgeable in the techniques of planning would do well to consult PPBS literature for the understanding it will afford of basic concepts.

Examples of plans set down are many and varied and many include such items as longer hours and strengthened staff, increased tax support, building program, addition of audio-visual materials, strengthened young adult program, additional services to children, service to hospitals, cooperation with all types of libraries in centralized procedures at state and regional levels, and total utilization of community library resources.

Planning is not a "single shot" activity. It is a continuing process and iterative in nature. It is well to keep in mind that this may include the possibility of entirely new ideas as well as ways to ensure the best utilization of resources and services now in existence.

Since the end objective of library service is to people, since people have been involved in the deliberations at every step, there is one final area in which people are of first importance. This is in the acceptance of the planning by the people, the citizens whom the board represents.

How Do We Get There?

The acceptance and support of the people for whom the board plans will make the achievement of the objectives possible. Essentially this involves communication. All the way through trustees must communicate, communicate, communicate.

And communication is half achieved if the community has been a part of the planning procedure. It was a wise man who said that "the greatest obstacle to effective communication is the illusion that it has been accomplished." Take nothing for granted when it comes to community understanding of what the library needs to make it a real center of education, information, and enrichment.

There are many ways to communicate, but there are two that are especially essential. One is in the political process at every level—local, state, and national. It means keeping in constant touch with government officials, giving service to them, and keeping them informed of the services of the library to the people to whom they are responsible, their constituency. Secondly, there must be a strong program of public relations. There should be, of course, the library's planned program of public relations. But equally important in public relations is the trustee telling the library story, utilizing every informal opportunity.

Summary

Library trustees and librarians are concerned with service to people through the institution of the library and their planning is to that end. Planning is a way of making sure that there is a strategy for library development always interpreted in terms of people. It is important to remember that library trustees stand or fall in their responsibility and public trust on what the individual user gets from the library. Trustees must recognize that the human element is paramount. The budget, building, or program are important as they affect service to people.

By examining where we are, where we want to go, and how we propose to get there, trustees have a basic structure for the planning process.

Libraries are essentially a product of change, and change is vital to their development. Planning is simply controlled change. How well trustees and librarians plan today, how well they instigate and control change, will determine the effectiveness of the library tomorrow.

Chapter Eight

Trustee Education

BY BARBARA B. HOLDEN

AND PHYLLIS MAGGEROLI

T RUSTEE EDUCATION includes every means by which the library trustee learns what his responsibilities are and how he can most effectively fulfill them. Experienced trustees as well as novices will recognize that trustee education must be a continuing process. Individual and group education are both valuable to the trustee, for as the individual becomes more knowledgeable his dedication and involvement in trusteeship will increase and he will find himself helping educate others.

Ideally, the new trustee will be given an introduction to his subject at his first board meeting, or even before, by his librarian and his chairman through the Trustee Orientation Program (Appendix I). If the orientation program is not offered, his own state association and state agency will still offer stimulation to and opportunities for learning. While there are usually librarians and other trustees who will provide the original orientation and who will continue to provide material for further education, trusteeship is finally a matter of self-education.

MRS. HOLDEN is a member of the New Hampshire State Library Commission. MISS MAGGEROLI is Special Programs Coordinator, American Library Association.

What the Trustee Needs to Know

What does a library trustee need to know? First of all, he needs to learn all of his responsibilities. He needs to learn the difference between the duties of a librarian and a trustee and to differentiate between their spheres of activity. He must come to know how to be informed, concerned, and supportive without being meddlesome.

He needs to know his library, both past and present—its legal basis, its finances, its physical plant, its policy, its collection, its staff, its services .

He needs to learn how his library is regarded in the community and to know that community—historically, demographically, economically, educationally, socially, and politically—in order to be able to relate community needs to library service and support. If his library is part of a system, then he needs to know the larger as well as the more immediate area.

His horizons as a trustee should, however, extend beyond the region of his own library. As a trustee, he should inform himself about both state and national library matters. He should familiarize himself with his state library laws and be aware of federal library legislation. He should discover his state library agency and the services offered by it. He should study the statewide plans for library development and consider how they relate to his own library, and how his own library is related to the larger picture. Familiarity with both state and national standards and statistics is a necessity if he is to have any basis for evaluation of his own library. Awareness of what is being thought and talked about and acted upon by librarians and trustees on both the state and national scene is certainly highly beneficial to effective trustee performance on the local level.

When a trustee makes a conscious and continuing effort to become educated in all these respects, the chances are not only that he will make a good trustee, but also that he will derive great satisfaction from his trusteeship.

Sources of Trustee Education

If the onus is upon him to further his own education, at least he has many sources to which he can turn. Not surprisingly, the first may well be his own library shelves. There are books and articles on libraries and trusteeship (See Appendix XI). Reading is an individual matter, and the trustee when initiated will choose for himself. Preliminary even to the present volume, however, will often be a shorter, simpler, more specific state handbook or manual prepared by the state agency, the state trustee association, or both. This is truly a basic text and should not just be read casually, but digested, absorbed, and referred to frequently. Library periodicals are also important. Most states and some multi-state regions have library newsletters or magazines. Sometimes these come from library associations, sometimes from state agencies. Regardless of the source, they are always *must* reading for area current events, and sometimes reflect significant ideas, trends, and regional developments. National library periodicals, such as *Library Journal, ALA Bulletin,* and *Wilson Library Bulletin,* will keep the trustee aware of the trends of library development on the national level. Also, all such publications frequently carry articles directed specifically to trustees.

Learning from Others

The trustee learns not only by reading but also by talking with librarians and with other trustees, by visiting other libraries, and by attending library meetings. To the new as well as the experienced trustee, library meetings may sometimes seem to multiply as rapidly as population in a backward country, but meetings are a necessary part of the continuing education process. Increasing knowledge, disseminating information, stimulating action, furthering cooperation, and exchanging experiences are only the more obvious benefits. From a planned or chance encounter at a meeting, many a trustee has been inspired with enthusiasm for a new idea or a new project from which has, in the long run, made all the difference to his library. And make no mistake about it, one trustee can in the final analysis make a difference.

Library meetings sometimes take place outside library associations, but the trustee who has joined his state, regional, and national organizations will have a broader field of action. He has an added bonus in the way of valuable reading material. For example, with membership in ALA and ALTA he will receive the monthly *ALA Bulletin* and the quarterly *Public Library Trustee* as well as other literature.

Trustees begin by attending meetings, institutes, and workshops. They go on to participate in them and so teach others as the trustees themselves continue to learn.

Group Education

From his local library orientation program and his own selected study of readings, the alert and interested trustee gravitates toward opportunities to deepen his understanding and increase his store of knowledge. Among these opportunities workshops are paramount.

Trustee growth will be accelerated through the stimulation of group learning. He can respond to other people's ideas, compare, select alternatives in the approaches to solutions of problems, and test his thinking against the thinking of others.

Through workshop experiences, many trustees have discovered the value of their contributions and have gone on to become gifted interpreters of the importance of library services.

Meetings and Workshops in the States

In a recent survey of state trustee associations and state libraries, there is ample evidence that most states use meetings and workshops as their chief means of furthering the education of the local trustee. These are often joint efforts of the state trustee association and the state library with an occasional effort including a library school as co-sponsor.

The workshops have covered a wide range of subject content. They have included duties and responsibilities of trustees, policy making, finance and budget preparation, cooperation, construction and remodeling of library buildings, public relations, personnel, library law, standards and statistics for evaluation of library services, the role and function of the public library, and the changing concept of public library services. Workshops at the informational level such as the duties and responsibilities of trustees predominate. Less frequently reported are workshops that have featured problem solving content such as "how to pass needed statewide legislation."

The meetings are varied in their patterns of frequency and length. The program planned for an annual state conference trustee gathering is the commonplace. These are one-shot meetings which usually permit no more than the superficial exploration of a single topic. Other programs include area, regional, and district meetings held once or twice a year ranging in length from one day to two and one-half days. Some states have experimented successfully with an evening series covering four to five weeks which focus on one or several topics of interest to the libraries in the area.

By far the most ambitious is the Governor's Conference which involves not only trustees but lay citizens representing a cross section of governmental officials, leaders in business, education, labor, communications, and librarianship. Some states have held a statewide conference, others have organized regional conferences or a combination of both. The Governor's Conference has usually focused on one major topic and explored it in depth over a period of from one to three days. The purposes of the conferences are of a broad nature. They seek to inform statewide leaders of the importance of library services in contemporary society, to describe the needs of libraries in the state, and to enlist the best thinking of the participants toward seeking solutions to the problems that hamper excellence of library service in the state. "Guidelines for Holding a Governor's Conference on Libraries, " by Mrs. Weldon Lynch, gives complete information on how to plan a Governor's Conference.

The report of state activity in trustee education, which has proved most effective, is one in which annual trustee workshops have been held with a planned sequence of content for continuity of learning experience. Each workshop has centered on an important theme and concentrated on it in depth. Then the next year another workshop has been held with content equally important to both the growth of the individual trustee and to the development of library service in the state. The long-range planning of these workshops creates cumulative learning and additional benefits with each year a trustee attends.

The workshops reported in the survey seem not to be restricted to trustees, but in some instances attendance by a librarian was limited to those who were accompanied by a trustee.

Attendance at workshops is sometimes discouragingly low. A help in this direction is now provided by the financial support being given through federal funds in states which have included trustee education in their state plans. Recognizing the large benefits from the educational experience, local library boards are giving more support to the attendance of their members to available workshops.

Reports from the states indicate that there is need for more coordination at the state level in the provision of trustee education as well as the need for more cooperation. In a very few states, a coordinator or consultant is employed at the state library to help develop long-range educational experiences for the trustees of the state. Such a person can provide continuity and coordination of effect in order to reach the educational needs of beginning trustees as well as the more sophisticated needs of trustees with greater experience. It can also provide for the fruitful interchange of knowledge between the different levels.

Planning a Workshop

Trustees sponsoring a workshop will find a planning meeting is the essential first phase. It is an important experience in group education for the planners. Also the needs of the group will be better met if the planning has involved representatives of individuals who will be at the workshop. All will benefit from the pooling of talents directed to the planning process and the exchange of ideas sparked from one member of the committee to another. Plans for the workshop will reap the advantage of the combined experience and knowledge of the committee members in writing objectives, selecting format and methods, assembling names and resources for the program, and allocating responsibilities to carry out the assignments.

The planning committee will find valuable assistance in "Planning Good Library Meetings," by Ruth Warncke. It describes the planning process in detail and gives an excellent checklist for selecting methods and program personnel, determining responsibilities for the details of meetings, and offers suggestions for carrying out the workshop plans.

The inexperienced planning group will find a helpful tool in the ALTA publication, "Workbook for a Successful Workshop," by Dorothy Corrigan. It is a step-by-step manual for designing a workshop tailored to the needs of a group.

A program planning group, particularly an inexperienced one, will do well to keep the plan for their workshop simple. Though the plan is kept simple it should never be dull. Simplicity in program planning is respecting the limitations of time, of potential program personnel, of resources of staff and money. It is far better to tackle one topic and treat it in depth than to plan a workshop covering too many subjects requiring far more than available time and talent will permit doing

well. Respect pacing in planning a program. No one is a good workshop participant who has been "talked at" too long. He should be
given a balance of opportunity to listen, absorb, react—to become
involved in the content of the workshop. Allow for the human limitation of the amount of information that can be absorbed in a single
session. The temptation is strong to pack in "just a little more" during a
scheduled time. Many a workshop session has had its effectiveness
diminished by the person who requested "a few minutes" to tell the
audience about "an interesting project."

Once a workshop format has been determined and all its separate
pieces designed to complete a pattern to carry out the workshop
objectives, stay with it. Workshops can be kept flexible and informal
but the close timing needed to make them effective requires that
informality be planned and organized, paradoxical as it may seem.
Changes requiring flexibility must be done with considerable expertise
and knowledge. The recreational portions of a workshop which provide opportunity for rest or informal chats with other participants
should be planned but not overorganized. The beginner plans his
program minutely and stays with it no matter how many enticing
bypaths present themselves.

To make sure the group has constructed the content to meet the
objectives set by the planners, test each session by asking "Which
written objective does this session meet?" Test the method decided
upon with relation to the goal of the session. Is this the best way to
present the information or elicit questions from participants? Has the
preparedness of the participants for this session's content been carefully considered? Do they need something more? A background paper,
a fact sheet, another set of opinions?

When the group is quite sure that the plan is good, that the objectives are the right ones, that the session content is designed to carry
out the objectives, that there is a variety of presentation methods, and
that a balance between receiving ideas and reacting to them is incorporated in the plan, *then and only then*, should program personnel be
selected. The most frequent error of all planning groups is to begin
with the suggestion of names for speakers. Resist, resist, resist the
temptation to think about who should be on the program before the
objectives are written and the program plan formulated. The program
personnel should be chosen on only one basis: Is this the best possible
person to do the job outlined?

The allocation and delegation of responsibilities for all parts of the program should be part of the initial planning meeting. The remainder of the job is the careful attention to details in carrying out the responsibilities. Whether the duties are to be in one or several hands, the most useful principle is "don't take anything for granted." Each person who has a job to do needs to have that job outlined, whether he has a major or a minor role. Briefing or instruction sheets should be provided.

As details of the program plan are carried forward, reality may dictate compromises and shortcuts. It is this reality that underscores the need for thorough work at the first planning meeting. The problems of implementing the workshop plan will likely be proportionate to the soundness and completeness of the original planning work done by the committee. The plan which has important objectives with sessions specifically prepared to meet them is the best guarantee for a successful workshop which gives an educational experience to those in attendance.

Trustee Education Benefits Libraries

In the final analysis, the ultimate aim of trustee education is to help bring about better library service for more people. The trustee who educates himself through the various media offered comes to realize a fuller sense of trusteeship and responsibility toward his own library in relation to all libraries.

Chapter Nine

The Trustee
and the Law

BY ALEX LADENSON

AND JUDGE STORY BIRDSEYE

A PRIMARY responsibility of a library trustee is to have a thorough understanding of the legal basis of the library board and the institution which he serves, together with knowledge of the responsibilities and limitations imposed upon him by law. He must also keep informed regarding current local, state, and federal legislation affecting the operation of libraries. While it is difficult for the average trustee to be aware of the many legal ramifications, statutory, judicial, and administrative, that are involved in the operation of a public library, it is vital that he be familiar with the basic legal concepts and principles.

Legal Bases for Establishment of Libraries

Library boards derive their governmental power from a variety of legal instruments. These take the form of general state library laws,

DR. LADENSON is Acting Librarian of the Chicago Public Library.
JUDGE BIRDSEYE is a trustee of the King County (Wash.) Library and Past President of the American Library Trustee Association.

city and county charters, municipal ordinances, special acts of the legislature, state corporation statutes including laws establishing educational corporations, and the state school code.

Because most of the public libraries in the United States are governed under a general state library law, it might be helpful to identify and describe the usual major provisions. One of the key provisions is a grant of power from the legislature to a local governmental entity such as a city, village, township, county, district, or region authorizing it to establish a public library. There are three different types of such grants. In some of the state laws, the grant is made to a corporate authority, that is the city council, village board, or county board of supervisors, authorizing that body to establish a public library. In other states, the general library law provides for a referendum of the voters to determine whether a public library is to be established. In still other states the law authorizes the establishment of a public library through a petition addressed to a corporate body, which has been signed by a fixed number or percentage of the legal residents.

Another key provision in a general state library law is the authorization to levy taxes for public library purposes. This grant of power to levy taxes, it should be noted, is made to the corporate authority of the local governmental unit and not to the library board, except in the case of certain district libraries which are expressly clothed with such power.

Finally, the third major provision in most general state library laws is a description of the plan of government for the public library. The law usually provides for a board of directors, trustees, or commissioners of a specified number, appointed or elected for a specified term of years, and enumerates the powers and duties of the members of the board.

Within this broad legal framework, it is now desirable to examine the powers and responsibilities of library boards and the limitations placed upon them.

Legal Power of Library Boards: Operating Policy

One of the fundamental powers of a library board is its authority to make rules and regulations governing the operation and management of the library. This is an important administrative power which has been delegated to the board by the legislature. Although the rules and regulations adopted by a library board are subject to judicial review (and this is true in the case of all administrative agencies), if the rules are reasonable, the courts generally will not interfere. It is under this power to make rules and regulations governing the operation and management of the library that the board of trustees is permitted to determine the service hours of the library, the schedule of fines for failure to return books, the amount of the nonresident fee, and similar matters. The board also has the authority to formulate the rules under which it conducts its official business.

Legal Power of Library Boards: Property Management

Another major power of a library board is the control, management, and care of all library property, real and personal. With respect to personal property, the library board enjoys exclusive control and possession. Regarding real property, however, there is considerable diversity of legal provisions and practice in the various states. Many library boards possess the power in their own right to purchase land and erect buildings; in the case of some other library boards, however, it is necessary to proceed through the intervention of the corporate authorities such as city or county to acquire land and buildings.

Library boards, although responsible for the construction and equipping of libraries as well as for their operation, generally do not have the power to issue bonds for this purpose nor can they levy taxes to meet the principal and interest on such indebtedness. This must be done by the corporate authorities, and in most cases a referendum of the voters is required before such a bond issue may be floated. The library board, to be sure, must take the initiative in requesting the bond issue and is responsible for mobilizing community sentiment in favor of the project.

In almost all states it is possible to acquire property for library purposes through the power of eminent domain. This is generally referred to as condemnation and requires the payment of fair and reasonable compensation to the property owner. Although there are a few states which have conferred this power upon library boards, in most jurisdictions this privilege must be exercised by the corporate authorities.

Legal Powers of Boards: Financing

Turning at this point to matters of finance, let us see what power the library board wields in this vital sector of library government. It is, of course, a primary responsibility of the trustees to see that the library is adequately financed. It is the board's duty to determine what funds are needed and what sums can reasonably be anticipated, to prepare budgets that are both sufficient and realistic, and to be prepared to explain and justify requests for funds. As a corollary it follows that trustees are obligated to operate their libraries within their budgets and on the funds made available to them.

By way of background, it is important to keep in mind that library revenue for operating purposes is almost always obtained through one of two methods: (1) from a special library tax on property usually expressed in terms of a millage rate such as one mill on the dollar of the assessed valuation of property; and (2) from a lump-sum appropriation from the general revenue of the municipality. Most of the states use the first method—that is, the millage rate.

It is quite clear that library boards, in general, do not have the power to levy taxes but are required to rely upon action by some corporate or municipal body. Nevertheless, they do have an important role to play in determining the amount of public funds that are to be used for library purposes and in fact this is often one of their greatest responsibilities.

In this connection it is well to observe that the state library laws usually contain provisions which fix either the minimum or maximum tax rate or both which a taxing body may levy for library purposes. Thus the Kentucky law, for example, provides that the tax rate for municipal libraries shall be not less than five cents nor more than fifteen cents on each $100 of assessed valuation of property. On the other hand, the California and Washington laws merely fix a maximum rate by providing that the tax levy for county libraries shall not exceed two mills on the dollar of assessed valuation. Many libraries in this country are not operating with the maximum funds allowed by law and, accordingly, this is an area which library boards might explore to advantage.

But whether operating funds come from a levy of taxes or from a lump-sum appropriation, the final decision as to amount is almost always made by others than the library trustees. Under such circumstances a most important consideration is the type of relationship that exists between the library board and the corporate authorities. If through the years the trustees have been successful in presenting the library's position to the town council, the county commissioner or the mayor in a persuasive manner, then the board should experience little or no difficulty in convincing the political power structure that a substantial tax levy or a generous appropriation is required. In interpreting the library to the corporate authorities and in obtaining adequate financing, the library board must employ political sagacity, diplomacy, firmness, and even the use of political pressure if necessary. There are many library boards that have established excellent working relationships with the municipal authorities and as a consequence they are virtually able to set the library tax rate to be levied or to determine the amount of an appropriation even though officially the levy or appropriation must be made by the corporate body.

In this connection it should be pointed out that in matters involving action by the state or municipal authorities, a prominent member of the library board can be of inestimable value because of his influence. Political scientists tell us that in modern urban society there are three major groups of men who control the governmental apparatus: (1) the elected officials; (2) the technical experts such as city and county managers, urban planners, public health technicians, public administrators, personnel specialists and the like; and (3) the economic and business elite. These three groups make up the power structure of the municipality. If the interests of the library are to be advanced, the library board must be able to establish an effective relationship and dialogue with this power system, and trustees who have contacts with its members should make appropriate use of their opportunities. Of course the library board must also have rapport with the voters at large, as it is the taxpayers who foot the bill. This is particularly the case when it becomes necessary to submit a proposed bond issue to a vote of the people.

In touching on the subject of library finance, one should not fail to mention the possibility of state aid. State aid for public libraries is based on the rationale that public education is a function of the state, and since public libraries are part of the educational system, they, like the schools, are entitled to financial assistance from the state. State aid, however, does not take the place of local support but is designed to supplement it. In those states where such help is available, library boards should be aware of the possibilities and should take advantage of them. In jurisdictions not presently affording state aid, serious effort should be made to secure the enactment of legislation designed to make such help available.

Legal Powers of Boards: Personnel

In the field of personnel, most state library laws grant the board virtually complete control over the library staff. This includes not only the power to hire and fire, but authority to establish new positions, provide job classification and salary schedules, and make promotions from grade to grade. As a matter of practice, the director is assigned the responsibility for the selection and supervision of staff as a part of his administrative duties. Where municipal civil service laws apply, the power of the library board in personnel matters is seriously curtailed.

Legal Powers of Boards: Inter-Library Cooperation

One additional area that must be mentioned is the power of a library board to enter into contracts with other libraries for the purpose of engaging in cooperative library activities. Most states have now authorized this and it is under such provisions of law that public libraries are now permitted to participate in the formation of cooperative library systems in joint ventures with other libraries involving the construction and operation of facilities, and in the pooling of resources. In fact, this development is one of the most promising legislative innovations of recent years.

Still another facet of library law is the enactment creating the state library and providing for its operation. State libraries are playing an increasingly important part in the library field and can be and are of great help to public libraries. All trustees should be familiar with their state library, with the services it provides, and with the many ways in which it can be of assistance to their own library.

Board's Responsibility in Federal-State Relations

In the last decade a monumental break-through has been witnessed in federal-state relations insofar as it affects all types of libraries. The

Library Services Act of 1956 strengthened by the Library Services and Construction Act and the substantial appropriation of federal funds, have opened up vast opportunities for the public libraries of America. There is also other legislation at the federal level that is of vital importance to the public library. It is clear that the federal government is beginning to assume its share of the responsibility for the improvement of public libraries. The legal basis for this federal concern is the "general welfare clause" of the Constitution. In *Minimum Standards for Public Library Systems, 1966,* the American Library Association declares:

> While public library service as a means of lifelong education is the responsibility of localities and states, the federal government should provide the necessary coordination and stimulation of this national resource as it does in the case of other matters of general welfare, such as schools, highways, and health.

It is essential that every library trustee have knowledge of the federal program and its possibilities. All library boards should take full advantage of the great opportunities open to them in this area. Library trustees, moreover, have an important role to play here in making their wishes known to the Congress in assuring that the program will be continued and adequately funded.

Trustees must also become imbued with the main objectives of the current library legislation, both state and federal. What this new legislation is helping to engender is the belief that books and ideas must move as freely in a democratic society as do vehicles of transportation. Municipal, state, and institutional boundaries must not be allowed to operate as barriers in the flow of books. New forms of library organization must also be encouraged to pave the way for an unimpeded and more universal exchange of books, information, and ideas.

An effective vehicle to insure adequate support and recognition of public libraries by state government is the adoption of a constitutional provision containing a declaration that it is the responsibility and concern of the state to provide for the establishment and support of public libraries which shall be available to all residents. Where a constitutional provision is not feasible, this type of declaration should be incorporated into the general state library law or into the statute from which the state library agency derives its authority. Michigan wrote such a declaration into its first constitution in 1835, and it has remained there ever since, even though there have been several revisions of this document. More states need to follow this example.

Finally, it is important to observe that law is not static or immutable, and that legislation does not originate in a vacuum. Law and legislation are deeply rooted in the social, economic and political soil of society, and reflect the changes that evolve in every facet of community life. For this reason it is vital that trustees seek to improve and expand legislation on a continuing basis, so that libraries can function more effectively and make a greater contribution to the educational and cultural life of this nation.

Chapter Ten

The Trustee
and Finances

BY CHARLES O'HALLORAN

I N A N age increasingly dominated by experts—space scientists, medical specialists, economists, planners—the layman faces complexities of immense dimensions in making right decisions and choices. Like Congress, a library board is a body of lay persons representing the citizenship, responsible to the citizenship for the conduct of public business. Especially in the field of finance, the board bears a serious public trust for the use of public money. Accordingly the library trustee—again like a member of Congress—should not hesitate to avail himself of the advice and counsel of experts for guidance and assistance in control of the library's finances.

The advantage of expert advice, however, is to help the trustee in making better-informed decisions, and does not in any way relieve the trustee of his individual responsibility to know and to act. Clearly spelled out in the list of the duties and responsibilities of the library trustee are two which cover the area of library financing. The library trustee must:

> Determine the purposes of the library and secure adequate funds to carry on the library's program;
> Assist in the preparation of the annual budget.

MR. O'HALLORAN is State Librarian, Missouri State Library.

As important as the expenditure of public tax funds may be, even more important to the library trustee is knowledge of the sources of such income, whether it be by appropriation or by tax levy. The trustee should be cognizant of ways and means of supplementing an income which has reached the legal limit: through investment, contractual arrangements with other libraries in the area, and through state and federal grants.

The Trustee's Share in Budget Making

In preparation of the library's budget, the expert operational know-how of the librarian and professional staff will furnish the board with necessary details. Fixed expenses of salaries, materials, maintenance and operation will be thoroughly scanned and discussed by the librarian and the board and carefully balanced against income available. Budget making for a public institution, as for any other public or private enterprise, follows the old adage of cutting the coat according to the cloth. The trustee must know what is involved in order to be of assistance to the librarian in preparing the budget for presentation to the appropriating body.

The trustee must be cognizant of the fact that financial needs, of necessity, grow out of the library's stated objectives, these objectives first being established upon a full and accurate knowledge of the needs of that specific community.

The trustee and administrative librarian then have recourse to state and national standards as guidelines for the achievement of these service objectives, such standards serving as well as a financial barometer of the likely costs of achievement.

Attendant to the preparation of the budget for any given year is an analysis of the answers to at least three basic questions:

1. How well has the library served its public in the year just ending?
2. How well is the library meeting its stated objectives?
3. What are the next implemental steps to be taken in order to achieve both short-range and long-range objectives?

The facts to be derived from an analysis of the answers should enable one to determine the cost in the year ahead of maintaining the existing standard of service and the gauging of the additional cost of bettering that standard in terms of additional staff, new materials, and programs.

Specifically, the trustee will be called upon to become familiar with myriad details. The provision of these details falls to the administrator, but their acceptance or rejection falls to the trustee.

Budget details, though voluminous, cannot be avoided. Priority will dictate, to a degree, the allocation of funds. Standards will suggest percentages for specific categories, but these can serve only as guidelines. They must be fitted to the local situation. Questions must be resolved: salaries over materials or vice-versa, for example. Is it better to have more materials in a kind of patron-help-yourself situation or less materials and more staff in order to more fully interpret and utilize the materials available?

Insurance, for another example, can become a real stumbling block. There are policies available developed and based upon library needs. These should be investigated. As in many areas, the trustee's state library or the American Library Association would be a conceivable information source on such matters.

The trustee should see that his library financial situation is readily understandable through the maintenance of an accounting system that is compatible with that used by the governing body from which the funds are received. The accounting system should provide a monthly check and, if not provided by the governing body, an annual audit should be made by a professional firm.

The alert trustee, briefly then, should follow a course of budgeting based upon pre-determined objectives, the implementation of those objectives each year, and an analysis of the past year's performance. Thus the library and its program will come to reflect a reasonable and justifiable improvement over its current status which will be in accordance with long-range development plans.

Although traditionally the library budget is prepared for submission at the beginning of each fiscal year, the trustee's responsibility toward it is continuing and year-round. The budget should be discussed at every board meeting, with the librarian reporting current expenditures to date at each meeting. There should be a continuing dialogue within the board of trustees, and between the board and the librarian, for informed examination of the ongoing program of the library. Current programs and long-range objectives must be questioned and justified in light of the library's finances. Changing situations may require revisions, which the board must be prepared to make.

Customarily, presentation of the library budget to the appropriating body is entrusted to the librarian and the chairman of the board.

Every trustee, however, must be exactly informed on every aspect of the budget in order to be prepared to share in its justification if needed.

Moreover, each individual trustee in his daily contacts must be prepared to answer questions about the library's expenditures. It is the right of citizens to question their representatives about their use of the tax dollar, and the trustee must be always alert to defend and justify the library program and operation.

Evaluation, Not Interference

The board's necessity for constant evaluation of the library program in light of finances available involves the individual trustee in a close study of the library's operation. But examination, questioning, even challenging current provisions of the budget do not give board members the right to interfere in the operation of the library.

Administration of the library is a clearly defined duty and responsibility of the librarian, and must be left within the province of the professionally-trained. An overzealous trustee, seeking in-depth knowledge, may all too easily intrude upon the daily operation of the library, unless he continually keeps in mind the line of demarcation between the duties and responsibilities of the board and of the librarian.

Looking Over the Financial Fence

The trustee's duty regarding financing of library operations does not at all preclude another important responsibility of the library trustee: the duty to plan creatively for the future program of the library. The board's constant watchfulness of expenditures versus income need not limit its vision of better library service.

Many a library, in fact, can date its first thrust toward modern library service to some boldly creative plan which was conceived primarily as an enhancement of the library's services by the board and the librarian, with the problem of "Where is the money coming from?" following as a matter of secondary consideration. The library board which never looks over and beyond its financial barriers may easily become over-cautious to the point of stagnation of the library's program. Boldness of concept calls for boldness of execution, and the forward movement of creative planning stirs up energetic efforts to find the necessary money.

Outside Funds and Financing

Outside funds not derived from the normal local revenue of the library are generally either state or federal funds. There are a number of federal programs which offer assistance to libraries; state assistance naturally varies in type and amount among the states themselves.

Detailed information concerning the federal programs of assistance to library service is set out elsewhere in this book. Complete information regarding state aid is available from the state library in each state.

It is well worth pointing out that since state library administrators coordinate statewide planning of all types of libraries, here again is an area in which the library board will do well to ask the advice of the experts. Once the local board and librarian have agreed upon a plan, consultation should be arranged with the state library agency for assistance both in working out the details of the program, and in obtaining the necessary financial aid.

State and federal support for library service can mean the difference between improved library services to the citizenship and the minimum service that results from "barely scraping by" financially. Rising costs of services and materials affect libraries as well as every other public institution and every private household. If limited local revenues require stringent economies and cutbacks in services offered by the library, it is the duty of the library board and the librarian to search for outside financing. Federal and state aid are designed to provide better library service to every citizen. The library trustee owes it to his library to be informed on this subject.

Trustees can be a real factor in continued financial support at the state and national level. They will find themselves in the legislative halls working for increased support for libraries. In these halls the competition for funds becomes intense as promoters of many splendid causes vie for the support and good will of the legislators. It is here that the trustee who has systematically analyzed and evaluated his own library's program, who knows and is committed completely to the values of that program, can, as a citizen, communicate effectively to the legislator who is himself a citizen. The motivation, understanding and commitment of the trustee and his communication to others are the keys to success.

Outside Financing Through Bond Issues or Local Taxes

Certain situations requiring outside financing for the library can be met by adoption of a local library tax, or by favorable vote on a bond issue. Such proposals are part of the political process which governs tax-supported institutions in this country, and the board of trustees should furnish enthusiastic leadership in these public campaigns.

Strong cooperation with the state library association is effective when the tax measure proposed is a statewide one. If the proposal in question is a bill favorable to libraries which comes before the state legislature, the library trustees, both individually and as a board, must be untiring in their efforts for increased financial support, through communication with legislators.

Gifts, Endowments, Bequests

An occasional source of outside financial assistance to libraries comes in the form of gifts, endowments or bequests. General recommendations governing acceptance and use of such benefactions are usually written into the library's policy by the board.

Consultation with the librarian and legal counsel from the board's attorney are also advisable, before the board makes a final commitment.

The Trustee's Philosophy Toward Finances

The very existence of a board of library trustees attests to the belief that a group of lay persons can and should determine the purposes, goals, and ultimate destiny of the public library.

At any point in time a library trustee possesses as his raw materials for work the accumulated traditions, practices, policies and material possessions of the library, and the right to make those decisions which in his judgment are important and necessary for the future of the library. Now is always a time for decision, with the past as a guide and the future a time affected by the decision. What happened in the past influences the decisions of the present and these in turn create the pattern of the future. These decisions are the responsibility of the trustee.

The one place where decisions made can be effectively implemented is the area of finance. Money makes things happen. The highest concept, the most brilliant project seldom comes about until somehow money becomes available to make it work.

The trustee, true to the democratic tradition of popular responsibility and possessed of the actual power to grant or to withhold funds, must be prepared to engage in a continuing, never-ending dialogue with his community, his fellow board members, and the librarian about the purposes and functions of the library.

The essence of effective library service—probably of democracy itself—lies in people who care enough to ask and to know, to plan and to execute, and to understand profoundly why. Upon the trustee who cares enough will rest the future of public libraries.

Chapter Eleven

The Trustee
and Building Problems

BY DOROTHY D. CORRIGAN

AND KEITH DOMS

Sʜᴏᴜʟᴅ ᴛʜᴇ children's room have a gay mural on the wall? Where should the new library be located? How do we get started? Who does what? How much will it cost?

Problems become questions with definable answers if an overall guiding philosophy is developed before a building program is undertaken. As a first consideration, the purpose, role, and goals of the library must be re-evaluated. In other words, just what is a library? This must be thought through carefully, discussed, and understood. All problems relate to this central question and add up to a single goal—the best library for the community. Only then is it time to consider the size and kind of building that will be needed to house the library collection and its services.

The modern library should be a place of wonder and curiosity and

---

MRS. CORRIGAN is Trustee Consultant for the Illinois State Library and Past President of the American Library Trustee Association.

MR. DOMS is Director of the Carnegie Library, Pittsburgh, Pennsylvania, and will be Director of the Free Library of Philadelphia (Pa.) September 1969.

beauty because truth and knowledge and human development are all discovered within the library. There should be dignity, warmth, and friendliness. The building should exemplify the spirit of library service. It should offer to the community a compelling invitation to enter, read, look, listen, and learn. The interior and exterior features should attain the functional efficiency and beauty found in the best architectural achievements.

A library orders, catalogs, stores, retrieves, and loans a wide variety of materials which includes books, magazines, films, phonograph records, pamphlets, maps, and pictures. The library staff helps people find out what they want to know and encourages a continuing education for all people.

Trustee Responsibilities

The planning of a library building is a team effort. The planning team includes the library board, the librarian, and the architect. An experienced library building consultant is often retained to assist them. The board of trustees must assign to the librarian the responsibility for the research and decisions in the many details which arise throughout the project. It must expect from the administrative staff recommendations on every phase of activity related to the program and the library service.

While each member of the planning team has well-defined responsibilities, the functions of the library board as the policy making body are fundamental to the entire effort for it is the library board that carries full responsibility for (1) initiating a building program, (2) organizing it, and (3) finding ways and means to implement the project. It is responsible to the community throughout the entire building project for legal and financial decisions and appointments. The specific duties of the board are as follows:

1. Make the decision that a new building is needed.
2. Select a qualified professional librarian to direct the service planning of the building program if one is not now employed.
3. Study the community.
4. Initiate a library survey.
5. Approve the written program of present and future building needs.

6. Direct the campaign to let the community know about the needs for a new public library building.
7. Appoint a strong building committee from within the board membership, or if small enough, name a committee of the whole.
8. Select and appoint a qualified architect.
9. Select and appoint a qualified library building consultant.
10. Select and appoint an attorney.
11. Select and appoint an interiors specialist.
12. Secure funds for the project if it is not endowed.
13. Estimate cost of operating the new building and seek assurance of adequate operating funds once it is completed.
14. Activate campaign, referendum, or whatever is needed financially.
15. Select and purchase a site with advice and assistance of the planning team.
16. Approve preliminary plans, furniture, and equipment layouts.
17. Authorize the invitation for bids for the building.
18. Approve construction contracts.
19. Approve furniture and equipment contracts.
20. Approve and pay invoices.
21. Arrange dedication, open house, and announcements to public.
22. Help acquaint public with the new services and program now possible and available.

The other essential members of the planning team are the librarian, the architect, and the consultant if one is retained. Generally speaking the librarian as the administrative head will coordinate all decisions related to the building project from inception through completion. He will prepare for the architect the written program statement of building and space requirements. This will be done after considerable research and consultation and with a continuous flow of ideas from staff, citizens, and trustees. The librarian should participate in all stages of the project.

The architect whose responsibilities are many and varied must provide all of the technical services required in the design, construction, and supervision of the project. The library board has a responsibility at all times to be in direct touch with the project through the librarian who is the coordinator. As the owner, the library board is constantly responsible to the government and community from which its authority is derived. As the administrative head, the librarian must be continually aware of his responsibility to the library board and through it to the community.

The building consultant will provide assistance with program statement, preliminary plans, site selection, equipment layouts, and other matters as may be required. He is usually an experienced library administrator who has been on the planning team for one or more successful building projects.

Community Study

A board of library trustees should not attempt to build a new library until it knows the community's needs and wants. Is the community growing? Changing? In what way? What groups and organizations are there? What are the educational needs? Business needs? Industry? Agriculture? Labor? Is there a junior college nearby? The answers to these and other relevant questions require professional knowledge of current community needs and future changes.

More specifically, what is needed is a careful analysis of the community the library serves, giving present and future growth trends, characteristics of the people, identifying other libraries and other recreational, cultural, informational, educational, and research facilities in the community. Are there existing plans for the area or regional library development to be considered? Are the results of any other studies available which may have been made about the library use or lack of library use in the community?

Studies of this kind can be done by a professional agency or agencies of government with professional surveyors. Occasionally local study groups undertake such studies. Clearly, the facts and information acquired will all be used as a basis for decisions affecting the building program. The building only exists to provide services and a program for the community and all the people who live there.

Library Survey

A library survey should be made whenever a new building is being considered. It can be undertaken by the head librarian, a qualified member of the staff, or a professional consultant in the library field from another community. The state library can be of assistance in providing suggestions of possible consultants. The purpose of such a survey is to evaluate all existing library services, review operating costs, and project program and space requirements.

Among the questions that need answers are: How does the library meet community needs now? What specific services are being given? What services should be added? Is the collection large enough? Is it sufficiently diversified? How well does the library compare with accepted state and national standards? Is there flexibility of planning for future unknown needs? Will the building serve as headquarters for extension and bookmobile programs? Will it be a part of a library system?

The library survey should include an evaluation of the book and periodical collections. There should be a complete assessment of the quantity and quality of audio-visual materials. The library staff should be evaluated in terms of qualifications, quantity, and duties to be performed by each staff member.

The results of this survey, together with the information obtained from community studies, will provide the facts on which the program for the new building will be based.

Library Location

While the library board of trustees has many legal, financial, and appointive responsibilities, selection and acquisition of an effective location is probably its most important responsibility once it has decided that a new building is needed.

Since it is intended as a service organization for the people, the library should be centrally located where it will be accessible to the largest number of potential readers and information seekers. What this means is that the library should be placed in the heart of a shopping center or business district, rather than in a remote location such as a park, civic center, or quiet side street, nor should a library be located where the noise or parking problems are primary considerations. The purchase of cheap land for the sake of stretching the building dollar is a false economy.

Despite widespread acceptance and ample documentation of this basic principle that a library must be located where there will be maximum accessibility for the greatest number of people, there are many officials, citizens, and businessmen who are not willing to recognize that it is penny wise and pound foolish not to purchase a site in the thick of things. Therefore, the library trustee must guard against pressure to accept a compromise location. Steps that a board can take to strengthen its position include sponsoring an objective site study conducted by an experienced library surveyor, reviewing professional literature on the subject, and making actual comparisons of effective locations with unsuccessful ones. The public libraries of Charlotte, Dallas, Atlanta, and Cincinnati are among those that enjoy excellent downtown locations. By comparison the Carnegie Library of Pittsburgh is located in an educational center three miles from the heart of the city, the San Francisco Public Library is in a civic center where practically all activity ceases at 5:00 P.M., and the Free Library of Philadelphia is isolated from the life of the city by a major expressway. Interestingly, there is very little difference in operating costs whether the library is in a good location or in a remote location.

There is no escaping the fact that it is up to the library board to choose and acquire the site for the library building. The technical and advisory services provided by librarian, architect, and consultant are invaluable, but in the final analysis it is the library board that must not swerve from its decision to acquire the best location possible even in the face of controversy and opposition. A Tennessee library board considered 25 different sites over a period of 19 months before it was able to acquire an effective location. The Norfolk Library Board was insistent that their library be centrally located. As a result, the library is strategically located in Norfolk's central business district.

Be it a central library or a branch library, a location which affords maximum accessibility to the greatest number of people is fundamental to the successful program of service of every new public library. Unquestionably, the provision of an effective location is a major responsibility of the library board that simply cannot be delegated to anyone else.

It should be noted that most library boards include within their membership businessmen, bankers, lawyers, and other citizens whose knowledge of the availability and value of potential library sites will enable them to assist real estate men and municipal officials in locating and evaluating properties that should be considered for purchase. In several communities, quiet investigation on the part of a few trustees placed the library board in a favorable position to negotiate successfully for valuable downtown property.

Financing the New Building

A financing plan needs to be developed and executed. This means identifying and studying all possible sources of finances. How is the

new building going to be financed? Local funds? State aid? Federal
assistance? Endowment funds? Gifts? New library buildings are usually financed by local government, most often through a referendum
and bond issue, or a special tax levy. Many fine public library
buildings have been built in recent years throughout the country with
little federal assistance. Sometimes endowments and special gifts can
be combined with other financing plans.

A very basic responsibility of the trustee is to see that the financial
support of the building program is assured. Campaigns for referen-
dums and raising the tax levy are specifically assigned to the library
board of trustees. Even when it is not necessary to have a bond issue,
it is vitally important that the community understand the need for a
new library building. Maximum and enthusiastic community support
should be stimulated by the board of trustees. Effective public relations and publicity will help create a good public library image.

The Board's Responsibility for Library Property

The public library is almost always a creature or instrument of local
government. As such, the parent government or the library board has
vested in it the power to purchase and appropriate property for the
purpose of erecting or enlarging public library buildings. Concur-
rently, the parent municipality or library board may hold property,
purchase, set apart or lease lands and buildings, or erect or alter
buildings for public library purposes.

In addition to the appointment of an attorney at the very beginning
of a library building project, if the board does not already retain an
attorney, careful study should be made of enabling acts, charters, and
ordinances affecting library buildings. Under certain circumstances it
may be necessary to pass local municipal ordinances for condemnation
or other purposes.

The Final Product

If the library board conscientiously fulfills its responsibilities, a new
library building will be erected which will provide the facilities required for a successful program of library service.

The building will be located where it will be accessible to the largest
number of people. It will feature street-level entrance and large

enough windows for passers-by to view its inviting interior. Its interior arrangement will be flexible with a minimum number of weight-bearing partitions. Lighting and year-around temperature control will provide personal comfort for readers. Furniture and equipment will harmonize with the architecture of the building and contribute to the library program.

Such a building, centrally located and arranged for convenient and comfortable use, will attract crowds of readers and information seekers of all ages, thereby assuring a maximum return on every tax dollar spent on public library service.

Chapter Twelve

The Trustee
and the Political Process

BY C'CEAL COOMBS

AND GERMAINE KRETTEK

T HE TRUSTEE and the political process are inseparable. Government involves every citizen. Governmental bodies control the regulations under which all citizens live—the education of their children, the right to live in the United States and to vote for the people who shall run it, to fight or to live in peace, to have dog leash laws, sewers, streets, and *the right to have libraries and to serve on their boards of trustees.* These governmental bodies at all levels make the laws and court decisions that permit the establishment of libraries and protect the freedom to read. But most significantly of all, they allocate the tax dollars that allow all of these services; indeed, that make it possible for libraries to be built, stocked, staffed, and operated.

Because it is a government of *all,* run by people elected or appointed through the franchise of all, government has come to be regarded as something which can be bent to achieve a desired end. There being

---

MRS. COOMBS is Vice-Chairman of the Washington State Library Commission and Past President of the American Library Trustee Association.
MISS KRETTEK is Director, Washington Office, American Library Association.

many diverse interests in present-day society, each brings to government its particular interest and each seeks to satisfy the needs of that interest. Thus an elected government is constantly being pressured by these diverse interest groups for favorable laws and ordinances and a bigger share of the tax dollar.

On the other hand, when political action is directed to the citizenship seeking the popular vote for a new tax or bond issue benefiting the library, any pressure employed must be channeled into a *selling* campaign—an intensified program of public relations aimed at establishing a favorable political climate for meeting library needs. Moreover, citizens who are thoroughly sold on the value and importance of the library will be more likely to express their convictions about the need for library support to governmental officials.

Library trustees, representing the library as a special interest group, have long found it necessary to be involved in interplay with other political leadership and with the public in general for achieving the specific purposes and goals of libraries. In spite of this necessary and historic involvement, many people even yet do not think of libraries as connected with the political process. Many, indeed, feel that libraries should be nonpolitical.

A much more realistic view is that libraries should be *nonpartisan*. The library can no more isolate itself from government—and, therefore, from the political process—than can any other institution, public service, business, or individual in today's highly organized society. New trustees, especially, are often disturbed by the prospect of political activity, believing it to be either futile effort or unsavory business. But it is a fact of life that if libraries are to survive as vital public institutions, trustees must make their voices heard above the competition.

The necessity for involvement in the political arena has greatly increased due to the pressing need for expansion and upgrading of library services and due to the mounting pressures by all areas of society for a part of the tax dollar. The scope of involvement has likewise taken on new and broader dimensions. While the primary interest of trustees is in their own libraries, they are now recognizing the influence which all areas of government have on library services and are witnessing the co-mingling of different types of library services. As they become more legislatively informed, trustees become more willing—indeed, more impelled—to assist at all levels of government for all kinds of libraries.

Effective Principles of Political Action

Some trustees are elected to their library boards; some are appointed. The powers and duties thus invested in them vary widely from place to place. Nevertheless, however varied the specifics, and regardless of whether the appeal is made to a governmental body or to the electorate as a whole, there are certain basic principles of political action which are universally applicable if such action is to be effective:

> A group desiring political action must work together and present a unified program.
>
> Whatever work is done must be through the existing power structure, retaining clear cognizance of the fact that often the people with the most influence may not be the ones holding the official titles of public office.
>
> There must be maintained year-round cordial contacts with all members of the power structure at all levels of government; and a continuing program of public relations strengthening the ties between the library and the public.
>
> In approaching a governmental body, it should be recognized that political battles are not won in the legislative halls, but rather through the influence of a "hard core" of citizen support that manifested itself long before the questions reached a forum of official action.
>
> Programs presented must be developed with well-thought-out and potentially feasible goals, possessing features of continuity and flexibility.
>
> Patience and a realistic outlook must characterize all political action and temper every sense of expectancy.
>
> Win or lose, thanks and recognition must be extended to all who aided in the efforts and doors must be kept open to all who didn't.

Specific Steps for Trustees to Take

Once committed to the necessity for political action and aware of the sound principles upon which it must be based, there are certain specific steps which trustees must take to achieve a successful program:

1. Establish clearly defined goals and objectives.
2. Document these goals in terms of
   (a) The current situation

 (b) How the proposed plan will improve the situation

 (c) What it will cost the taxpayer.

3. Set up a time table. The need for action may come sooner than expected!

4. Prepare a concise but complete program statement in printed form for wide distribution.

5. Present the program formally and informally, being sure to include personal contacts, the importance of which cannot be exaggerated.

6. Rally public support. In appealing to the electorate, this is a *must*. In approaching a governmental body, public approval is a necessity—political leaders, even when in favor of a program, find it difficult to implement one without a strong demonstration of public support.

7. Utilize all information media. Know that newspapers, radio, and television are essential to any campaign for civic advancement, including libraries. Telephone calls or personal visits to media officials usually result in better news coverage.

8. Continue to communicate with key people throughout the period of political action.

9. Follow through on any questions or requests that are made.

10. Remember to say thanks and to give appropriate recognition for all assistance received.

Successful Trustee Action in the Political Process

The degree of success which is being achieved by trustees on the political front varies from place to place and from time to time. Success comes in direct proportion to the adherence to sound principles of political action and to the expertise and thoroughness with which the necessary steps for political action are taken. Though much remains to be done, libraries are making significant gains.

It is worthy of note that where gains have been made, trustees have been active on the political front. They have acquainted members of governmental bodies and the public with present library programs, unmet needs, and plans for the future. The importance of the library program has been clearly explained to city, county, state, and federal governmental bodies. Through political action of this type, trustees have helped government accept its responsibility for financial support of the library, and this in turn has assisted in obtaining a legal structure favorable to library development.

To be effective in political action, trustees must recognize that such activities are implicit in their responsibilities of trusteeship. Politics is everybody's business, and it is up to the library board to set the political tone as it relates to libraries.

A sound basis for political action requires that objectives of the library program must be acceptable to the public and to governmental bodies. Therefore, in cooperation with the librarian, the board must clearly identify the goals sought. Proposed improvement programs should aim at meeting specific library needs, including both short- and long-range objectives. Have continuity of each proposed improvement as an extension of a previous one, and consistency with local, state, and national goals for library service. Imagination, vision, and proposed innovations to meet library needs have a strong appeal, but the board must remain basically realistic in keeping the library program related to the other needs of the community. The fact that improvement of all services takes additional staff, materials, and buildings—which in every case means additional financing—must never be forgotten.

Once the board has arrived at agreement as to the objectives to be pursued, it is well to formulate a basic written policy to guide and support the positions taken. A working outline with a time table will be helpful, as it should be kept in mind that timing of political action must be related to the schedule and agenda of the legislative body to be approached, or, in the case of a general election, to the local election laws.

Approach to Legislators

Approach to the legislative body should be carefully thought out. Each city, township, county, region, and state, as well as Congress, has its own particular government form and methods which must be understood. If the politically alert library board has kept up live and interesting contacts the year around with mayors, councilmen, commissioners, governors, legislators, and congressmen, the trustees will have no difficulty in reaching these representatives when legislative action is needed.

Once action is started with any legislative body, follow-up should be constant until objectives are achieved. It is well to be realistic about what can be expected or achieved in any one session from any legislative body, so that if any specific appeal is unsuccessful at first attempt, there need not be undue discouragement, but rather a willingness to keep trying. Whether successful or not, trustees should always keep in mind that the members of a legislative body are friends as well as authorities, and that the proper relationship with them involves respect, sincerity, and appreciation.

Ways to Communicate with Legislators

Meaningful communication with congressmen, governors, state legislators, county commissioners, councilmen, and government agency representatives is absolutely necessary to successful political action. Meetings, letters, and telegrams can swing the balance in favor of the library, if carefully thought out and properly used. The following is a useful check list of what to do and what to avoid in these contacts:

MEETINGS

DO . . .	DON'T . . .
Meet often with elected representatives	Make it a formal occasion
Be prepared; have facts and proposals at hand	Make it a purely social occasion
Present facts clearly—prepare a one-page fact sheet	Talk in generalities (Be specific!)
Give acceptable alternatives to the proposal	Ask for unrealistic promises
	Forget to inform your own members
Put the problem on a local basis	Ask the sponsor of the bill to support the measure (He already does)
Invite the official to a question-and-answer session with your group	Forget to explain library needs in terms of human resources
Be prepared to answer questions and arguments against the proposal	Forget to be friendly and enthusiastic
Meet with candidates before the election	
Meet with winners after the election	
Remember to say "thank you" often!	

LETTERS

1. Know *whom to write*—the sponsor of the bill, legislators, members of Congress, county officials, councilmen, commissioners, members of committees who consider the bill.
2. Know *when to write*—keep informed; time letters according to legislative action. Use the official designation for the bill and refer to its title or content to identify it.
3. Know *what to say*—the letter should be complete, clear, concise, correct, and courteous. Officials' voting records can be no better than the information available to help them make decisions.

TELEGRAMS

DO . . .	DON'T . . .
Remember that telegrams have been overused by pressure groups	Send unless absolutely necessary
Apply same rules as to letters	

Appealing to the Electorate

Perhaps the broadest field of political contact in which trustees work is in their daily contacts with individuals. This constant public relations program by trustees as representatives of the library should pay high dividends as a powerful force in favor of the library when those individuals go en masse to the polls on voting day. Trustees who are constantly aware of their responsibility to sell the library and its needs have found a higher expectation of success when the time comes for a public vote on a bond issue or library tax.

The strongest public support comes from citizens with knowledge of and appreciation for the library. The library board overlooks no opportunity of meeting with and inviting in citizens and organizations for presentation of the needs and plans of the library. Their cooperation and support should be invited in furthering the library program.

Trustees successful in political action know that a wide-range public relations program should be followed using all types of communications media: newspaper articles, newsletters, house organs, flyers, radio and television programs, speakers before organizations and groups, face-to-face conversations, telephone calls, telegrams, folders of factual materials, invitations to meetings and special library functions, and rides on bookmobiles. All these offer channels through which to present the shortcomings of present library facilities strongly enough to establish immediately the need for expansion and improvement—then to concentrate on selling the taxpayers the advantages of what the new tax or the new bond issue can offer. Library board members should constitute themselves an informal speakers' bureau to carry the library message to clubs, groups, and civic organizations.

In this field of political action, perhaps the most important single aim is the final step of getting out the vote. The most favorable pre-election acceptance of library appeal is useless unless backed up at the ballot box. Trustees, aided by the Friends of the Library and other interested individuals, should spearhead a concerted drive to get out the vote. If the citizenship has been throughly sold on the advantages of library improvement, their favorable votes will express that acceptance.

But vigilance is the watchword. The trustee who is politically aware will never relax throughout the pre-election campaign of selling the voters on the issue of meeting library needs—nor, indeed, can strenuous political action be relaxed until voting day is over and the polls are closed.

Points to Remember in a Library Campaign

As there are certain specifics to bear in mind in communicating with members of a legislative body, there are similar points to remember in a campaign designed to appeal to the public:

DO . . .	DON'T . . .
Accentuate the positive	Sell the library short—even to prove a point
Stress the advantages of the library proposal	
Appeal to civic and community pride in the library	Berate the taxpayers (Voters respond more favorably to persuasion.)
Make the library appeal to the *total* population	Try to conceal the cost of the proposal to the taxpayer (Offset costs by future benefits.)
Take advantage of every opportunity for favorable publicity	Overlook the power of "just one vote" (One vote could turn the tide!)
Enlist the aid of every library-minded citizen, especially in getting out the vote	Take success for granted (No election is won until all the votes are counted!)

Summary

In brief, the key to trustee success in the political process lies in willingness and ability to:

Acquire knowledge of the total political process
Adhere to the sound principles of effective political action
Ascertain the present and future needs of libraries
Develop plans to meet these needs
Act within the political process to obtain the means to satisfy these needs.

Chapter Thirteen

The Federal Government and the Public Library Trustee

BY RAY M. FRY

H AS THE community outgrown its Carnegie library? Could a new children's room be built by remodeling unused storage space? If only the library had enough money, would it not be possible to launch a special demonstration program of service to the disadvantaged, or to develop a communication link with special library collections in the state?

These and other questions concerning the improvement of public libraries can very likely be answered by help from federal grant programs. Since 1956, the federal government has provided funds specifically for public library service. The largest program of benefit to public libraries during this time has been the one enabled by the Library Services and Construction Act. There are many other federal programs, however, which provide funds, but do not mention *libraries* in

MR. FRY is Director, Division of Library Services and Educational Facilities, Bureau of Adult, Vocational, and Library Programs, U.S. Office of Education, Department of Health, Education and Welfare, Washington, D.C.

their titles; work is sometimes necessary to discover which programs can benefit libraries. Programs and approaches for problems facing library trustees are pointed out in this chapter.

Library Needs and Government Support

Certainly the world today is a complex and changing one. A social revolution and an information and publications explosion are taking place. Public libraries, like all educational institutions, are evolving, not static. They are influenced by and need to respond to the educational and social changes of today's society. There is a new urgency in serving the disadvantaged; in making use of all the newer media such as films, microforms, teaching machines, and television; and in providing better library services through systems or networks of libraries.

Today there is more cooperation and sharing of responsibilities among the local, state, and federal levels of government. Effective working relations between the different levels of government are basic to providing adequate library services for all citizens. State library agency administrators are the leaders responsible for statewide planning of all types of libraries. The role of the trustee can be very important in making the governmental process work.

It may be said that Congress looks at federal educational grant programs as either short-term incentive programs or as long-range continuing programs to solve special national problems which can be accomplished only on the federal level. The continuing everyday support of education in the United States is assumed to be primarily the responsibility of state and local governments. Congress has voted support of new approaches to help solve long-standing problems in the area of public library services and information services. This support is designed to bring services within the reach of every citizen, including the physically, culturally, and economically disadvantaged, so the talents and potentials of all individuals and groups in our society can be used.

Federal Grant Programs

Public Library Buildings

The problem of providing modern up-to-date library facilities is one touching both the urban and rural segments of the population. Funds under Title II of the Library Services and Construction Act (LSCA) can be used for the following: (1) construction of new buildings, (2) additions to existing buildings, (3) renovation or alteration of existing buildings, and (4) the purchase of existing buildings. A local library which has money for matching funds under this program can apply to the state library administrative agency in the state capitol for participation in this grant program. States set forth their own priorities for awarding construction grants under the LSCA and incorporate these priorities into a written state plan.

The state library administrative agency in each of the fifty states, the District of Columbia, and the outlying areas, prepares a comprehensive state plan to qualify for participation under the LSCA program. This state plan makes provision for programs for public library services, public library construction, interlibrary cooperation between various types of libraries, state institutional library services, and library services to the physically handicapped. The state plan is then submitted to the U.S. Commissioner of Education for approval. The determination of the best use of the funds under an approved state plan is reserved to the states and their local subdivisions.

In addition, multipurpose federal financial assistance is available for the construction of public facilities in different areas of the country. The Public Works and Economic Development Act of 1965 makes provision for grants and loans for communities designated as Economic Redevelopment Areas. Communities in Appalachia can secure money to be used as matching funds assistance for certain federal programs, including Title II of LSCA, from the federal program of Supplemental Grants-in-Aid for Appalachia under the Appalachian Regional Development Act of 1965. The Demonstration Cities and Metropolitan Development Act of 1966 makes provision for general supplementary assistance for library construction in specified urban areas.

Public library trustees should also be aware of the availability of surplus property through a program administered by the Office of Surplus Property Utilization in the Office of Assistant Secretary for Administration of the U.S. Department of Health, Education, and Welfare.

In Rhode Island there is an exciting example of how federal programs can work together to construct a facility and enlarge the usual concepts of a public library. The planned Blackstone Valley Area

Library received federal funds under Title II of the Library Services and Construction Act and a supplemental federal grant from the Public Works and Economic Development Act through the New England Regional Commission. All federal funds are being matched by state and local funds. When completed, this public library facility will be the central library for the three Rhode Island towns of Woonsocket, Cumberland, and Lincoln. It will eventually become a science resource center for the northeastern part of the state and is expected to extend its services by contract to adjoining areas of Massachusetts. Planning for this area library was done in coordination with the existing academic, public, school, and special libraries in the area. This area library will be a supplementary resource center for all libraries in the area.

Public Library Services

The emphasis in providing any type of library service is on the consumer—the person who wants information and publications. First, methods for improving services to him within the local library might be considered, and second, services between libraries.

Title I of the Library Services and Construction Act authorizes grants to the states for promoting the further extension of public library services to areas without services or with inadequate services. The state plan is developed which includes a section on public library services. Local libraries apply to the state for participation in the state's annual program under the state plan. Local libraries, individually or as members of library systems or cooperatives, can estimate needs in their areas for the following: bookmobile service to places which do not have library service; increased reference collection and service; special collections of large-print books for persons with vision problems; a separate section and collection of books, records, and posters in the library for young adults; a circulating record collection; films and projectors which can be borrowed by civic groups or individuals; framed art reproductions; additional trained personnel to work with children, young adults, and adults; or a program for the disadvantaged persons in the library service area. These and many other ideas can be implemented with federal help.

One successful example of service to the culturally deprived is a demonstration program being conducted by the Los Angeles Public Library with LSCA Title I funds from the California State Library.

The program is focused on services to persons of all ages within minority groups in specified areas of the city. The project was launched in 1965 and has increased library contacts in culturally deprived areas of the city. Project staff members go into housing projects and by using the direct person-to-person approach convince individuals that the library has something of value to offer them.

The public library and the public library trustee should make certain that every segment of the population under its jurisdiction is served. More specialized learning needs, such as braille books for the blind and overhead viewers for the physically handicapped, have too often been neglected. These special needs can be met with federal funds under LSCA Title I or more appropriately under Title IV, Part B, which deals with library services specifically for the physically handicapped, including the blind.

After considering how to build up library services from within, the board should consider how the library can cooperate with others to serve the community. Cooperation among all types of libraries—public, school, college, university, and special, as well as information centers—is the goal of LSCA's recent Title III, Interlibrary Cooperation. The local public library can seek participation in this program with the state agency as it does in those programs mentioned above for services and construction under LSCA. With appropriate funding and good leadership, this new title has unlimited potentialities for cooperation among libraries. It is designed to bring *total* library services to all Americans.

Personnel

Almost every public library needs more and better trained professional and nonprofessional personnel. Jobs are becoming more specialized and salaries are going up. Fellowships at the master's, post-master's, and doctoral levels are available for graduate library school education under Title II-B of the Higher Education Act of 1965.

Workshops and institutes are another way of keeping library employees up-to-date about new techniques and ideas. Many state library agencies sponsor workshops with funds under LSCA Title I.

It is often more feasible to send staff away for a one- or two-week institute than for a long period of study. Beginning in 1968, institutes for librarians working in public libraries are being held all over the country, funded under Title II-B of the Higher Education Act. These institutes are for persons serving in professional library positions, regardless of their training. These institutes provide intensive training in various fields of study, including: oral history, map librarianship, materials and programs for the Spanish surnamed, expanding public library service to the culturally and economically disadvantaged, and government publications. Federal funds cover tuition, a stipend, and a dependency allowance for each participant; they do not cover travel expenses. Institutions of higher education receive federal grants and make awards for these institutes. The continuing education of public librarians and their staffs should be a matter of direct concern to all trustees.

The preceding is a condensed version of federal grant programs affecting public libraries. There are many more federal programs not mentioned above aiding other types of libraries.

Other Federal Library Services

Federal libraries themselves provide services to all libraries. The most significant perhaps are those of the Library of Congress, the National Library of Medicine, and the National Agricultural Library. The maintenance of various national union catalogs as well as the catalog card distribution and cooperative cataloging activities of the Library of Congress are indispensable services to American libraries. The Library of Congress' automation of its bibliographical apparatus, including the production of catalog records on machine-readable tapes, will affect almost every library. The Library of Congress has operated the National Books-for-the-Blind Program for over 30 years. Legislation has now extended this service to include persons who cannot read conventional print because of physical handicaps other than blindness.

The complete range of federal government activities relating to libraries goes beyond library grant programs aiding all libraries. All these benefits cannot be sufficiently described here. An adequate account would include details on the Depository Library Act of 1962 through which certain libraries (many of which are public libraries) are designated depositories for U.S. government publications. It would discuss federal exemptions and privileges for libraries, such as the special library postage rate which applies to the mailing of books, records, films, and other materials to or from libraries and nonprofit organizations; and services of the Smithsonian Institution such as the

National Gallery of Art's film loan, traveling exhibits, and sale of color reproductions.

Library administrators are probably best sources of information on federal programs in connection with libraries and information services, especially the operations of the U.S. Office of Education. USOE administers: the Library Services and Construction Act (the direct administration of LSCA has been decentralized to the nine DHEW regional offices); the academic library resources and the library fellowship and institute programs under Title II of the Higher Education Act of 1965; the school library resources program under Title II of the Elementary and Secondary Education Act of 1965; and the library research and demonstration program, under Title II-B of the Higher Education Act, in which public libraries are among the eligible institutions for research grants.

The chart at the end of this chapter is a comprehensive listing of federal programs which have either direct or indirect implications for the development of public library services. It omits the usual headings of "amount of appropriation" and "where to apply," because dollar amounts and agency addresses tend to change with the lapse of time. The chart is used to indicate the *kinds* of federal assistance programs which should be kept in mind by an alert public library trustee.

Steps Trustees Can Take

Steps that a trustee might take to learn sources of aid to help his library meet its needs:

1. Know how your library or library system measures up to the generally accepted national library standards. Have your library administrator give a realistic overall evaluation of your library situation—its collection, personnel, and financial state.

2. Know your community, being particularly aware of the parts of the population such as the people in rural and urban areas that have made little use of library resources and services. Be acquainted with other library facilities in your area. Consider with the other members of your board and your librarian possible interactions and cooperation between the various types of libraries.

3. Think in terms of total library services which will require co-

operation between several types of libraries and greater use of newest automated techniques.

4. Know the priorities for immediate and future library needs of your community.

5. Know the organization of your state library agency which administers programs that can aid your library. It is especially important to understand how your own state library agency operates, since most of the federal programs are state plan programs and are therefore administered by the state. Be certain that your state library agency is adequately staffed and supported to handle constantly increasing responsibilities.

6. Know the federal programs and how to get additional information about them. Give your own local library administrator and/or appropriate library staff "time and travel" to keep up with federal programs. Attendance at the right conference or a trip to see a new project may cost the library "peanuts" compared with the ultimate benefits they can derive from seeing successful programs in action.

7. Plan ahead for your library. Planning is a complex matter which normally requires reaching beyond the local library staff to the more specialized knowledge of staff from your state library agency or other consultants.

8. Promote your library plan and its implementation. Public library trustees can often speak more effectively than librarians about the need for library development.

9. Participate in trustee meetings and library conferences and workshops at the regional, state, and national levels in order to be aware of current trends and programs in library services. Governor's Conferences are particularly valuable because they are geared to the library situation in your own state. (This same participation applies, of course, to your library administrator and his staff.)

10. Accept the challenge of change and be prepared to play a key role in librarianship of the future.

Summary

Federal programs have become increasingly important to public libraries. With adequate funding, accomplishments under all Titles of the Library Services and Construction Act can be outstanding. This legislation has already brought new or improved public library services to over 85 million persons, some of these receiving such services for the very first time in their lives. Nationally accepted standards—particularly those of per capita financial support—still represent only a distant goal for the vast majority of public library systems, however.

Perhaps the most important factors for the public library trustee are knowledge of his own community and library, an understanding of federal aid programs, and a close and cooperative working relationship with his local library administrator, his state library agency, and his state library association. The strength and range of interests of the state library association on concerns such as federal assistance programs accurately reflect the current status of library services in that state.

The key to improved and expanded library service is often to be found in the many federal aid programs available. It is the trustee's responsibility to study and understand these programs of government support for libraries and to use this valuable key to better library service.

DIRECTORY OF LEGISLATIVE PROGRAMS

I. For Public Library Construction

Types of Assistance	Legislative Authorization	Administering Federal Agency
1. Construction of new library buildings or purchase of existing buildings	Library Services and Construction Act (P.L. 89–511, as amended), Title II, Public Library Construction	Office of Education Department of Health, Education, and Welfare Washington, D.C. 20202
2. Additions to or remodeling of public library	Library Services and Construction Act (P.L. 89–511, as amended), Title II	Office of Education Department of Health, Education, and Welfare Washington, D.C. 20202
3. Surplus real property available to educational agencies including public libraries	Federal Property and Administrative Services Act of 1949 (P.L. 152, as amended)	Office of Surplus Property Utilization Department of Health, Education, and Welfare Washington, D.C. 20202
4. Funds which can be used by local agency to meet matching requirements of other federal programs	Appalachian Regional Development Act of 1965 (P.L. 89–4)	Appalachian Regional Commission Washington, D.C. 20235

Based on the chart in *ALA Bulletin* article of October 1967 titled "Federal Library Legislation, Programs, and Services: II"

Types of Assistance	*Legislative Authorization*	*Administering Federal Agency*
5. Supplementary grants-in-aid to other federal programs	Public Works and Economic Development Act (P.L. 89–136) Title I	Economic Development Administration Department of Commerce Washington, D.C. 20230
6. Construction costs for certain branch public libraries may be used as off-setting credits in favor of municipal contributions	Housing Act of 1949 (P.L. 81–171, as amended)	Department of Housing and Urban Development Washington, D.C. 20410
7. Interest-free advances to states and local government for planning essential public facilities (including public libraries) within a reasonable time period	Housing Act of 1954 (P.L. 83–560, as amended)	Department of Housing and Urban Development Washington, D.C. 20410
8. Long-term loans for construction to assist in the finance of needed public facilities	Housing Amendments of 1955 (P.L. 84–345, as amended), Title II, Public Facility Loans	Department of Housing and Urban Development Washington, D.C. 20410
9. Building multi-purpose neighborhood centers in low-income neighborhoods. Priority is given to situations where local Community Action Programs, under the Economic Opportunity Act, are already under way	Housing and Urban Development Act of 1965 (P.L. 89–117, as amended), Title VII, Community Facilities Program, Sec. 701–703	Department of Housing and Urban Development Washington, D.C. 20410
10. Purchase of land up to 5 years in advance of proposed construction to encourage communities to acquire land in a planned and orderly fashion for future construction	Housing and Urban Development Act of 1965 (P.L. 89–117, as amended), Title VII Community Facilities Programs, Sec. 704a, Advance Acquisition of Land	Department of Housing and Urban Development Washington, D.C. 20410
11. Supplementary assistance to meet matching requirements of federal construction (and to some degree service programs) for libraries that have program components in demonstration cities	Demonstration Cities and Metropolitan Development Act of 1966 (P.L. 89–754, as amended) Title I, Demonstration Cities	Model Cities Administration Department of Housing and Urban Development Washington, D.C. 20410

Types of Assistance	Legislative Authorization	Administering Federal Agency
12. Supplementary grants for federally assisted development programs of cities	Demonstration Cities and Metropolitan Development Act of 1966 (P.L. 89–754, as amended), Title II, Planned Metropolitan Development	Office of Intergovernmental Relations and Urban Programs Coordination, Department of Housing and Urban Development Washington, D.C. 20410
13. Extension and improvement of public library services	Library Services and Construction Act (P.L. 89–511, as amended), Title I	Office of Education Department of Health, Education, and Welfare Washington, D.C. 20202
14. Systematic and effective coordination of the resources of school, public, academic, special libraries, and special information centers through establishment and maintenance of local, regional, state, or interstate cooperative networks of libraries	Library Services and Construction Act (P.L. 89–511, as amended), Title III, Interlibrary Cooperation	Office of Education Department of Health, Education, and Welfare Washington, D.C. 20202
15. Improvement of state institutional library services	Library Services and Construction Act (P.L. 89–511, as amended), Title IV-A	Office of Education Department of Health, Education, and Welfare Washington, D.C. 20202
16. Improvement of library services to the physically handicapped	Library Services and Construction Act (P.L. 89–511, as amended), Title IV-B	Office of Education Department of Health, Education, and Welfare Washington, D.C. 20202
17. Provision of training and retraining programs to equip persons for work in needed employment fields	Manpower Development and Training Act of 1962	Office of Education Department of Health, Education, and Welfare Washington, D.C. 20202
18. Captioned film loan program to provide cultural and educational services to the deaf	Captioned Films for the Deaf (P.L. 89–505, as amended)	Office of Education Department of Health, Education, and Welfare Washington, D.C. 20202
19. Programs for the disadvantaged; support educational programs in areas having high concentrations of low-income families	Elementary and Secondary Education Act (P.L. 89–10, as amended), Title I	Office of Education Department of Health, Education, and Welfare Washington, D.C. 20202

Types of Assistance	*Legislative Authorization*	*Administering Federal Agency*
20. Support of supplementary educational centers and services, including literacy programs for adults	Elementary and Secondary Education Act (P.L. 89–10, as amended), Title III	Office of Education Department of Health, Education, and Welfare Washington, D.C. 20202
21. Strengthening of community service programs	Higher Education Act of 1965 (P.L. 89–329, as amended), Title I	Office of Education Department of Health, Education, and Welfare Washington, D.C. 20202
22. Library research and demonstrations	Higher Education Act of 1965 (P.L. 89–329, as amended), Title II-B	Office of Education Department of Health, Education, and Welfare Washington, D.C. 20202
23. Surplus personal property available to educational agencies including public libraries	Federal Property and Administrative Services Act of 1949 (P.L. 152, as amended)	Office of Surplus Property Utilization Department of Health, Education, and Welfare Washington, D.C. 20202
24. Grants to states to help communities plan and coordinate programs for older citizens through agencies such as libraries	Older Americans Act of 1965 (P.L. 89–73, as amended), Title III, Grants for Community Planning, Services and Training	Administration on Aging Department of Health, Education, and Welfare Washington, D.C. 20202
25. Government publications available to designated depository libraries which make the depository materials available for the free use of the general public	Depository Library Act of 1962 (P.L. 87–579)	Superintendent of Documents U.S. Government Printing Office Washington, D.C. 20402
26. Community action programs for upgrading community services and resources for low-income residents	Economic Opportunity Act of 1964 (P.L. 88–452, as amended)	Office of Economic Opportunity Washington, D.C. 20506
27. Project grants available to public libraries for the interchange of information and public understanding and appreciation of the humanities	National Foundation on the Arts and the Humanities Act of 1965 (P.L. 89–209, as amended)	National Endowment for the Humanities Washington, D.C. 20506
28. Planning for public library development as a component of a comprehensive regional plan, including library planning	Housing Act of 1954 (P.L. 83–560, as amended)	Department of Housing and Urban Development Washington, D.C. 20410

Types of Assistance	Legislative Authorization	Administering Federal Agency
29. Librarian fellowships and traineeships (Master's, post-master's, and doctoral)	Higher Education Act of 1965 (P.L. 89–329, as amended), Title II-B	Office of Education Department of Health, Education, and Welfare Washington, D.C. 20202
30. Institutes for persons serving all types of libraries	Higher Education Act of 1965 (P.L. 89–329, as amended), Title II-B	Office of Education Department of Health, Education, and Welfare Washington, D.C. 20202
31. Provision of part-time employment for young people to help them begin or continue vocational training in public libraries as part of a work-study program	Vocational Education Act of 1963 (P.L. 88–210, as amended)	Office of Education Department of Health, Education, and Welfare Washington, D.C. 20202
32. Part-time and on-the-job training for students of high school age from low-income families in all businesses, including libraries	Economic Opportunity Act of 1964 (P.L. 88–452, as amended), Title I, Part B, Neighborhood Youth Corps	Office of Economic Opportunity Washington, D.C. 20506

Chapter Fourteen

The Library Trustee
and ALA Standards

BY LOWELL A. MARTIN

In the long run it is the informed and committed layman rather than the professional administrator who determines the quality of public service. This applies to long-standing facilities such as schools and roads and to emerging needs such as pollution control and urban renewal. It applies equally to public libraries.

The layman determines the quality of public service in part by the amount of money that he provides. But prior to money is what the public really wants. If the people want better schools and better libraries, the money can be found in the American economy.

In standards, as in other tenets of library administration, the trustee is the connecting link between the institution and its public. One way to conceive appointment as a library trustee is as a commission to answer three questions for the public: how good is our library—how good should it be—what needs to be done? Out of this commission

DR. MARTIN, a library trustee in Metuchen, N.J., and a member of the lay advisory board for the New Jersey State Library, is a professor at Columbia University, School of Library Service.

come the three responsibilities of the trustee in connection with library standards: he should know what they are—he should apply them to his own library—and then he should carry the word back to those who commissioned him.

The Present Standards

The thrust on the part of professional librarians for better library service through formal standards goes back several decades. The essential documents have been national statements of the American Library Association. Various states have adopted or modified the national pronouncements, either in direct formulations of state standards (California and Wisconsin, for example) or embodied in statewide library plans (New York, Pennsylvania, and Illinois, for example). Localities have then "applied" the standards to their own facilities, either by studying the state and national documents and using those portions judged relevant to their situation, or by ignoring the formal standards, this last being a negative action which also has an effect on quality of service, a little like not voting for a political candidate or a bond issue.

For present purposes we need to trace the national statements back only to the *Post-War Standards for Public Library* (1943). This document had some impact on librarians and modest impact on trustees, and contributed to a post-war stirring about for means of improvement. The 1956 statement, *Public Library Service, a Guide to Evaluation with Minimum Standards,* combined the push for excellence with the growing concept of library "systems" as a way to improve library service jointly among several governmental jurisdictions and over large areas. Followed shortly after its publication by federal aid to public library service, which was used in considerable part to further the same concept of "systems," the 1956 document became part of the working background of many librarians and some trustees, and influenced both state plans and local efforts. In 1967 the earlier statement was updated and revised, while retaining much the same theoretical basis and organizational structure.

The trustee's homework on standards should start with this recent publication, *Minimum Standards for Public Library Systems.* Actually it is in two parts, the document proper, and then a financial supplement which presents sample budgets embodying the recommended standards (under the title "Costs of Public Library Service 1968" and appearing in the October, 1968 issue of the newsletter of the Public Library Association of ALA, *Just Between Ourselves*). In addition the American Library Association has issued more specific statements of standards for smaller libraries, children's service, young adult service, and bookmobiles.

Library literature is neither exciting nor poetical, so one hesitates to propose additional reading to the trustee, but there are two related statements of library standards that deserve at least one evening of scanning. One is the parallel ALA document on standards for state libraries, *Standards for Library Service at the State Level* (1963). While part of this deals with internal facilities in the state capitol, the bulk of the content relates to individual libraries as part of the state structure for service. The other statement worth a little attention is the forthcoming *Standards for School Media Programs*, which points the way for the future for school libraries. The public library trustee will be struck in the school document by the emphasis upon multi-media service—in fact the term "library" is seldom used.

The reader will note certain common properties among the several ALA publications. Rather than being bare listings of standards, each is based on underlying principles which are set forth, thus giving the philosophy behind the specific recommendations. This is an asset for the trustee, because he is better able to judge the justification for the standards. In all three documents there is more stress on qualitative than on quantitative criteria, although an effort is made to pin down some specifics in statistics. The sparsity of exact numerical standards may leave the trustee uncertain at times, but this characteristic of the national pronouncements has the virtue of making them more flexible and adaptable.

The essence of the public library statement is conveyed in its title, *Minimum Standards for Public Library Systems*. The standards present a floor and not a ceiling. And they apply not to each small, separate library, but to groups of libraries working together to achieve better library service cooperatively and jointly. Here is a challenge to the trustee, to think and plan for his region and not just parochially for his local library—at this point he has an opportunity to lead the way in inter-governmental relations in his area.

After the national statements come the library standards of the individual states. These too are part of the body of measurement against which the trustee will seek to judge his own library. A few states have formalized their library standards and in these the trustee can get a distinct publication for study. But don't be put off too easily if you are told that there are no separate standards in your state. Is there a state plan for library service, and if so, what are the aims and criteria on which it is based? If no formal state plan, is there state financial aid for libraries, and if so what are the assumptions on which it was designed and the formula for its distribution? Such formulations reveal or imply standards even if their authors did not consider them as such. And if the trustee is told that in his state there is neither a state plan for libraries nor state aid to share in the cost of libraries as part of the educational program, he might well ask why not.

As the lay trustee reads the various standards documents, he will naturally inquire as to who prepared them. The answer is primarily professional librarians. Trustees did participate in the committees which composed the public library statements, but they were in a distinct minority. The standards are essentially the credo of national library leaders. They can back up their recommendations by pointing to libraries that have achieved many of the standards and are clearly strong and effective agencies, and to others that fail to come up to the criteria and show self-evident shortcomings. But the lay person will be conscious that he is reading a tract prepared by interested parties concerning an institution to which they have dedicated their lives. This should make for respect for the credo, for it comes from full commitment and long experience. But the trustee equally should watch for untested assumptions in the statement and for technical stereotypes that can characterize professional thinking.

This suggested attitude toward outside standards is not an excuse for any individual trustee or board of library directors to *lower* them, unless they can first show that their clientele is less in need of lifelong education than people living elsewhere. The trustee's contribution to library standards could be more to raise or broaden or deepen them, going beyond the "standard" professional outlook. Nor is this an invitation to disregard certain standards because they challenge an existing library or open up unfamiliar or uncomfortable prospects. Thus, rejection of standards for access to more specialized resources is not justified because a library is small—on the contrary it is all the more reason to seek out systems membership in order to open a channel to such resources.

The reading of the standards statements, even the studying of them, is not the end of the exercise for the trustee, but just the beginning. To this stage he has taken the first step, that of being informed, but it remains to apply the standards and then to take action on them. In the first step of becoming informed about standards the trustee has merely been a good pupil, studying the lessons prepared by the American Library Association; now he becomes a participant in preparation of standards for his own locality and the surrounding district.

How Good Is Your Library?

Appointment to a library board comes as something of a surprise to many trustees, and they take on the assignment wondering just what their responsibilities will be. It shortly becomes clear that the board has certain obligations under law and certain interests by custom. Board meetings are devoted to these matters, and constitute the "business" of the group. Beyond regular meetings there may be some committee work of a near-administrative nature, and this seems to be the sum and substance of the job. After all, there is a paid, full-time professional staff, and a responsible director, and most trustees soon recognize that they would do well to keep out of management activities.

But this is likely to leave a void, both in the mind of the trustee and in the development of the library. The chief librarian seeks to deal with the state of the institution in his reports and implies it in his recommendations to the board. But the thoughtful trustee still wonders. Actually how does our library measure up? He listens and he asks questions. How good should it be? At this point he has his own values but he hesitates to impose them on an agency for all the people.

The application of standards is a juncture point of the professional judgment of the librarian and the community knowledge of the trustee. Both views are needed to reach a valid appraisal and a program for the future; both are needed in deciding which among the many standards should be given priority in the local situation. The trustee brings a value judgment and a community identification which must be reflected in basic evaluation and in setting standards for development. Indeed this is why there is a library board at all. It may be that many administrative decisions taken in board meetings could as well be made by the librarian alone; it is in considering how good the agency is and how good it should be that a lay group has a clear contribution to make.

Joint attention to standards, by the professional and by the trustee, should therefore be consciously planned. This essential task should not be left to chance or to a few relaxed and seemingly inconsequential moments at the end of the board meeting.

It is instructive, as a starter, to bring standards into the board sessions on a small scale. Pick out one or two of the recognized criteria and ask at a meeting just how the library measures up. The chief librarian may be defensive at first, feeling that his stewardship is being challenged, but most professionals are quick to seize a chance for constructive review. Individual board members may initially be unsure whether this is a legitimate topic on the agenda. But as the librarian offers what evidence he has they are likely to be drawn into the discussion. Differences in viewpoint will emerge. Probably it will be found that additional information is needed. The board will be doing what it was set up to do, considering where the library is and where it should be going. And individual members will go home feeling that they are engaged in something equal to their talents and to which they can contribute, rather than rubber-stamping indicated professional decisions.

In time the trustee will have a much clearer conception of his own library. He will have not only his own good sense and good will on which to depend, but also an objective set of criteria. This will stand him in good stead in dealing with specific questions that come before the board. It will help him in considering budget proposals. When the occasion arises to seek out and select a new chief librarian, he will have a sharper focus on what kind of administrator his library needs.

Most important, the application of standards to the agency for which he shares responsibility will guide the trustee in planning with his colleagues for the future development of the library. If in time he comes in the process to recognize the limits of planning for separate, individual libraries, and is pushed by his concern with standards to participate in regional, state and national developments, library service will have gained an effective champion and the individual trustee a worthy cause.

Without a sense of institutional goals, library trusteeship can be at best routine and at worst frustrating. Standards can be the means to see beyond the board resolution of the moment and to rise above the provincialism of each trustee's opinions.

Improving Standards of Service

People in general have no ready basis for judging library service as they do for some other facilities. A highway, they know, should be smooth and straight and fast. The standards are self-evident and they are relatively high. If proper standards are not achieved—when traffic backs up or the roadway has pot holes, for example—the motorist knows that something is wrong and he has no hesitation in voicing his opinion.

But how fast and smooth and straight should his library be—that is, how many books should it have, of what quality, backed by what skills in the library staff? The average library user has little basis for judgment. If he gets what he wants he is grateful. If not, he often feels that he can't really expect the agency to suit his individual needs. Public library service is patently weak in many localities—it is remarkable how little public criticism one hears of these faltering agencies.

The trustee is the one who should know where his library stands. If he has done his homework, he is informed about library standards. If he is committed, he wants high quality for his community. If he has done his job, he had determined where his library comes up to standard and where it falls short.

But this knowledge on the part of the trustee is not just private information, nor simply background to be used solely at board meetings. He in substance has been appointed to find out how good the library service in his community should be, and once he finds out he should take the message back to the public. This starts with budget sessions before the appropriating body, when the trustee better than the librarian can tell elected officials what the library should have. It extends to formal presentations before civic and cultural groups—each trustee should have a ready speech, not fancy or technical but informed and sincere, on "How good is our library," and he should give it before the businessmen's groups, and the political organizations and the various civic and educational groups. Informing the public of library standards even extends to informal contacts in the community, over the back fence and across the dinner table.

What should the trustee do about library standards in his own community? He should work to improve them. What should he do about library standards in his area, beyond the borders of his own municipality? He should work with trustees in nearby jurisdictions to improve the total level of service, in the self-interest of readers young and old in his own town. These are the reasons why he is a library trustee.

Chapter Fifteen

Library Systems

BY JOHN A. HUMPHRY

AND RUTH E. POLSON

Library trustees have had experience with their home town library. Now they are recognizing the need to increase its efficiency and to strengthen and expand its services by helping to create library systems. A library system is defined as "an association of autonomous local libraries or a group of branch libraries working together to improve library service for all residents of a county or multicounty area."[1] While particularly evident in the case of public libraries, the system concept is also being applied to academic, school, and special libraries within a given geographic area. The enormous increase in the demand for information, the proliferation of knowledge and the competition for the tax dollar have helped pave the way through a variety of organizational patterns to these new formations. For example, the Division of Library Development in New York State now administers state aid of 15½ million dollars annually to support its 22

---

[1] The New York State Library. Division of Library Development. *A Primer of Public Library Systems in New York State.* Rev. ed. 1967, p. 7.

MR. HUMPHRY is Assistant Commissioner for Libraries, New York State Education Department.

MRS. POLSON is a trustee of the Finger Lakes Library System, Ithaca, New York.

110

public library systems. In 1968, they included all counties in the state and served 99 percent of its population. Library systems have proved their value and are now a fact of library life.

Benefits of Systems

Interlibrary Loan

A natural first question arises, "What are the benefits of a library system?" A frequent response from trustees is that through this mechanism the total resources of a library system are made available to users wherever they live. To be specific, interlibrary loans make possible securing particular book needs, i.e., certain authors, titles, or subjects. For example, a businessman wants more help in management or accounting. A preacher seeks ideas for his sermons. A housewife wants new ideas for decorating her home or feeding her family. A scoutmaster wants information on nature study. A ghetto dweller wants to find out how to start a housing cooperative. A university professor wishes to see the most recent critical study of Dante.

Fresh Materials

Systems benefit member libraries by adding fresh materials to collections. When new books and other library materials appear among the tired familiars, both patrons and librarians rejoice, circulation rises, word-of-mouth publicity increases, and new users venture into the library. Nearly any unit can substantiate the fact from its own experience, but a telling example comes from a small library in a satellite town of Buffalo, New York. Long stagnant, it finally, hesitantly, joined the regional system. The system for three successive years added $2,000 worth of new books, attractively processed, to the formerly dormant local collection. Meanwhile the new librarian culled ragged or nondescript volumes from the shelves. People who had never approached the library began dropping in to see what was happening. Recently, an open house was held in a handsome new building. Of course, other factors helped to maintain the continuous growth, but new books—conspicuously evident—caught public attention and gave the first big impetus.

While no system can pour $2,000 worth of new books for three successive years into every one of its member libraries, it can achieve comparable results through rotating collections or other loans from a central book pool. That is why systems arrange for some major regional collection of 100,000 or more volumes in areas where an existing large library does not supply such a source.

Only sizeable book "banks" can simultaneously permit adequate circulation to their own customers while sustaining the burden of multiple withdrawals from member affiliates. And only through access, via the system, to such a book "bank" can small libraries provide the ever increasing numbers of fresh books and other library materials needed by their patrons.

Strengthened Collections

Although patrons may be originally attracted to libraries by a display of new titles, they will seldom keep on returning unless they continue to feel rewarded for their effort. It is not enough to capture their attention. Here systems make one of their finest contributions to local libraries. They strengthen local collections. Particularly, reference and non-fiction sections are reinforced because they tend to be seriously inadequate and outdated. The present emphasis on scientific matters puts a premium on timely data. Many scientists and technicians report that outdated information nowadays can be not only time-wasting but also dangerous. They urge the use of more periodicals as one way to solve the time gap between discovery and dissemination. Here systems broaden both the quantity and the quality of local provisions. Frequently, too, they open the door to acquiring non-book materials. Thanks to system stimulus even little libraries can offer their communities access to phonograph records, television and film programs, maps, and microforms. These relatively new library services are especially helpful in initiating services to the disadvantaged and enriching educational-cultural programs.

Advisory Services

Closely paralleling the help to their collections, systems offer advisory services to member libraries. In fact, many of the new reference works might get inadequate use if systems did not train local staffs in their content and applications. Often, too, the enticing fresh materials would be diluted were the shelves not carefully weeded first of outworn, non-circulating items. Untrained librarians especially seek guidance in this function.

As the whole educational-library complex expands in our modern society, many local libraries find they are outgrowing their buildings. Again, system consultants can be requested to advise on space requirements, programs, plans, and equipment. Where new construction is financially impossible, they can be ingenious with suggestions for renovation. Meanwhile they can nurse more ambitious projects to completion. Today few systems are legally permitted to contribute directly to capital construction costs, but they can act as channels to federal funds available under Title II of the Library Services and Construction Act. However, most systems can and do contribute generously to such new equipment for their member libraries as shelving, catalog cases, storage cabinets, charging desks, tables, and chairs.

More important perhaps than improvement of the physical plant is the broader scope of local library services. System consultants are repeatedly called in to advise on starting new services. Surprisingly many libraries are just instituting provisions for children and young adults. System consultants suggest ways of coping with the student influx or advise on services to the disadvantaged. They answer appeals for assistance with programs for organizations in the community and for senior citizen, racial or religious groups. All in all, system advisory services are in high demand.

Communications

Usually, when a system is formed, one of its first needs is to establish various kinds of communications among its members. Some kind of regular delivery service is imperative. This may be a truck, use of the mails, or any local vehicle that can move library materials from one member unit to another. A Canadian library uses dogsleds, and there are some places where delivery by boat is the only practical solution.

Besides the necessity for sending and receiving library materials, system members need rapid access to each other to exchange book orders and interlibrary loan data. Hence most will need telephones as a minimum communications device. These systems often install or subsidize long distance calls, at least until their usefulness is demonstrated to their smaller members. Of course, large units will also be joined by the more sophisticated machinery available today; teletype or telefacsimile.

Since so much of the successful operation of local libraries and systems depends on good public relations, systems promote such activity among their members. This can include everything from book lists and posters, programs for National Library Week and other occasions, to speakers' bureaus, films, and television specials. All the printed media naturally are pressed into service. Drama, radio interviews, street wagons, and store-front centers are just a few of the many public relations tools promoted by systems to tell the library story.

Monetary Savings

While interlibrary loans, strengthened collections, advisory services, and communications appeal widely, trustees are also interested in monetary savings made possible by systems. First of all, pooling the book orders of members results in appreciable savings because the discount rate becomes higher. Again orders are the choice of the individual members, quite free from system influence. Many systems establish centralized cataloging and processing to avoid expensive duplication among members and to free the time of local librarians for more immediate services to the public. Various bibliographic aids, such as book lists and union catalogs, result in major savings in search time and costs for interlibrary loan requests. Best of all in the eyes of many libraries are the various grants that many systems give outright to their members. These may be book grants, cash grants, or scholarship funds. The latter have encouraged a number of young people to enter training for a professional library career.

New Services

The proportionately greater financial and other resources of a system allow for imaginative applications in new services. System funds may provide a new reference consultant, say to help students in particular or merely to make the collection more meaningfully available to the general public. One system hired a special trustee consultant. Her job was to lend continuity to trustee orientation in her area. Another system, heavily weighted with small libraries manned by untrained volunteers, hired one professional to circulate in a concentrated fashion among first one group and then another of these little libraries in much the same way as a rural preacher serves several churches. This librarian stays several consecutive weeks in each locality as opposed to the in-and-out trips of the regular consultants. This permits in-depth familiarity with local situations and patrons.

Many systems either initiate or help support expensive services, such as framed art collections with supporting educational colored slides or complicated new services, such as government documents or microfilming important local historical documents. Also, to help member libraries be more aware of all their obligations, they may promulgate services to people in health, welfare, and correctional institutions.

Services to Rural Sections

In addition to the assistance public library systems offer to established libraries they perform an important function in getting library services to sparsely settled areas. They may set up deposit stations—a small collection of books left in a community, administered by a local patron, and changed from two to four times a year. Or they may work with local residents to create a reading center—a more ambitious project, still short of a chartered library, in which the area citizens contract with the system to supply such wants as rotating book collections and consultant help in setting up a catalog and starting children's services. Or they may operate a bookmobile—a traveling library carrying from 1500 to 3200 books, pictures, films, and phono discs. Generally a professional librarian, as well as a clerk and a driver, is on board to help with reading guidance and to take orders for interlibrary loans. Or, of course, where the conditions warrant it, systems will help local citizens establish a permanent library.

Services to Trustees

Last, but by no means least, systems provide important training for trustees. Even though each chartered library is a legal unit, there are still local trustees who are vague about their legal rights and responsibilities. They need explanations and assistance in methods before they can adequately run their own units. This becomes of paramount importance as the local libraries affiliate in systems. Now the home town trustee must manage his own unit so that it will mesh properly with the system network. He may also be called upon to serve as a

board member for the system. This demands mastering legal responsibilities of broader scope, handling more money, and somehow raising
his library sights above the familiar provincialism of his local library
horizon. Systems provide this kind of training. They also have opportunities for much wider and more meaningful training. There is a built-
in challenge in the wider scope and greater finances available because
of systems. Trustees are ready to respond. Systems can help them
acquire a basic core of library information. This will not only make
them more efficient in their own right but also will assist in making
possible better cooperation between librarians and trustees.

Organization and Administration of Systems

Kinds of Systems

Because of the great variety of conditions and laws under which
libraries operate in the different states, the structure of public library
systems and their governing boards also vary. A metropolitan library
serves a big city and may cover one or more counties. Normally, it
forms *a consolidated system* with its branches. The branches are
financed and administered under the direction of the central unit. The
board of trustees takes office and operates under the charter or law
that permitted the library. This may mean it is appointed by a city
council or a county board of supervisors or is designated by a state
charter. The board sets policies, secures funds, and carries out sundry
other legal responsibilities for the system.

Under other conditions, a group of libraries within a county may
form a *federated system*. Each keeps its autonomy, continuing its local
finances and board of trustees. The county appoints a superstructure
board to receive county funds and service the federation. Local units
may contract for special services and exchange materials through the
county federated board. Strengths of the local units may be shared
more widely and county funds may bolster the usually inadequate
local appropriations.

However, the most wide-spread and popular type of system today is
known as a cooperative or area library system. It extends over several
counties or other political units. Again, local libraries retain autonomy
and continue with their usual board of trustees and financing.

Organization

While the early library systems included only public libraries, in recent years systems of academic libraries, systems of school libraries, and special information networks, such as those involving the medical libraries, have been established. The opening of the Ohio College Library Center to perform bibliographic services and to share specialized resources is recognition of the fact that college and university libraries face the same problems as public and special libraries in providing all the services and resources an active academic community needs.

In 1966, the newest system concept of library service in New York was instituted and is known as the Reference and Research Library Resources Program, or to use the more popular term, the 3R's. It is built upon the public library system structure, and its purpose is to assist serious users of library materials to identify, locate, and gain access to them through a chain of resources.

In some states, notably Massachusetts, the library agency designates a central library as a headquarters library to administer the system and to serve as its resource center. The service areas include a number of county libraries in the plan of service. Trustees helped assemble data, talked with officials and legislators as participants in devising and implementing these plans. Other states are devising systems that embrace all types of libraries that cooperate regionally in providing more sophisticated levels of services.

Library systems should become part of a worldwide communications and information network which will embrace not only all types of libraries but also the whole gamut of information retrieval systems using the most advanced computers and machine technology.

Financing

Once systems have been examined for their usefulness and structure, the next obvious area to explore is finance. Local tax and endowment funds have been the traditional support for libraries. Yet, even in the case of single units, as political, social, and economic factors have evolved, library demands have increased beyond the ability of these sources to meet such demands. Today, so widespread are the needs for library services that the support of other governmental agencies is needed to carry the enormous financial burdens and to spread the costs equitably. Systems are one element in that financial total.

Until recently circulation or per capita figures or some combination of them have been used to establish library support levels. These are no longer valid. Partly this is true because the two most emphasized thrusts nowadays of the expansion of library services, namely, services to the disadvantaged, at one end of the spectrum, and to the scholarly researcher, at the other end, happen to be the most expensive services libraries offer. Also, costs in general have risen and the shortage of professionals pushes salaries higher during competitive bidding. Hence, leaders in the library profession as well as the American Library Association itself stress the need for operating budgets for libraries and library systems based on criteria other than established figures of per capita expenditure. Even a high per capita expenditure does not necessarily provide an adequate library budget. It is essential, therefore, to expend sufficient sums to meet library standards promulgated by the profession.

As libraries work toward meeting these standards, quality service can become a reality. Quality service means a library should:

(1) Be open a sufficient number of hours daily to insure an opportunity for all who wish to use the facilities.

(2) Own a book collection providing authoritative information in all fields of knowledge, representing community interests, for all age groups, showing evidence it is being added to regularly and judiciously weeded and which includes recordings, films, and other modern communication media.

(3) Employ a staff properly trained to interpret the book collection to its constitutents.

(4) Be housed in an attractive, functional, and inviting building.

(5) Pursue an effective public relations and public information program.

Once having ascertained their desired library standards, trustees need to use all their resourcefulness and ingenuity to see that sufficient funds are allocated to meet them. As has been explained, this now involves the participation of all levels of government. Trustees need to join with library professionals in attempting to devise a formula to be used as a guide in determining the fair share to be borne by federal, state, and local governments in support of library service. Then all can rally to the gargantuan task of providing such funds.

Shortcomings of Systems

Systems have provided tremendous impetus toward the betterment of library services. Evidence is overwhelming in their favor. Still, they are a new concept and tool and need further refining. Financing them properly presents problems. Because of the historically uneven development of library services, sticky jurisdictional frictions arise where a poor district abuts a good one. Straddling both financial and jurisdictional problems is the need for sustaining metropolitan libraries as they struggle to realize the fine service potential of their magnificent collections without going bankrupt. Trustees tend to think of huge libraries as having inexhaustible financial backing. Actually their needs are as great as their responsibilities. At this point in library history they are facing financial crisis. All libraries lean heavily on the grants, but system stimulated demands have pushed this pressure to the danger point. How to keep large libraries viable is of acute concern and affects trustees and librarians in units of all sizes.

From these overwhelming problems to picayune affairs involving minor adjustments in the details of cataloging or processing, systems demand greater awareness of others, less provincial outlook and more unselfishness. These are not easily achieved, so systems in this sense may be said to generate some frictions. However, a perusal of the New York State comprehensive evaluation of its *Emerging Library Systems*[2] (for public libraries) leaves no doubt that the shortcomings of systems are minor compared to their great and positive contributions to library service. What seems indicated for the future is that building on this exhilarating experience the system concept will be expanded until there are no limitations on the area served nor on the type of participating libraries or information agencies involved. To quote the report itself,

> "Traditional attitudes and approaches notwithstanding, as the problems become broader and more complex; as the need for research, innovation and experimentation becomes greater; and as the tools of

[2] The University of the State of New York, The State Education Department, Division of Evaluation, Albany, New York. *Emerging Library Systems*. The 1963–66 Evaluation of the New York State Public Library System. February 1967.

the library profession become more sophisticated; there is a growing need to move to broader bases for leadership and planning, as well as for the support of public services. Library service has quickly and irreversibly moved into a three-cornered partnership among local, state, and federal government. Its future welfare will depend on how willingly preconceptions are laid aside and how successfully plans are developed which assign to each of these partners that portion of the job which it, and it alone, can do best."

Chapter Sixteen

The Trustee
and Library Automation

BY DANIEL MELCHER

I N THE fall of 1965 the librarian of Sydney, Australia, paid a personal visit to most of the United States libraries which had been getting publicity about their automation programs, and found next to nothing that was in any sense operational, let alone economic. His survey report, financed by a Carnegie Traveling Fellowship, was summarized in the *Library Journal* of January 15, 1967.

If he were to repeat his 77-day tour today, it is unlikely that he would find many more "successes" though he would surely find more "interesting experiments" as they are generally called when they don't pan out quite as hoped.

Cynical though it may sound, one of the greatest services a library trustee can render his library, be it large or small, is probably to take a hard-nosed, "show me" attitude when automation is proposed. It is conceivable that the proposed automation is valid for libraries (or at least for this one) and that the would-be automaters could carry it through successfully—but on the record of recent years the chances

---

MR. MELCHER is Past Chairman of the R. R. Bowker Company and has served as a trustee of the Montclair (N.J.) Public Library.

are heavily against it. The number of people who have had successful experience in automating library procedures are few indeed.

Published Reports Available

In 1968 the ALA began publishing, through its Information Science and Automation Division, a *Journal of Library Automation.* It is perhaps appropriate to note that in the first three quarterly issues only one public library project was described—and this was a project under contemplation, not one actually in operation.

In its annual report the Washington University School of Medicine Library reported 1967–1968 as "the most frustrating year" of its planned automation of acquisitions and cataloging, despite the fact that when the year began "all the budgeted positions were filled with either librarians who had worked with computers, or computer technicians who had worked in libraries for some years." Problems included staff turnover, a change of computers, and failure of efforts to work jointly with the main library.

Must reading for any library trustee confronted with a decision about possible automation is the article, "Trial by Computer," by Basil Stuart-Stubbs in the *Library Journal* of December 15, 1967. It's fiction and it's funny—but the truth in it will make you wince. It's supposed to have happened in a college library, but never mind; the relevance to public libraries is close enough.

Evaluation of Place of Automation in Library Service

It is unpopular and unfashionable these days to do other than bow and scrape when automation is mentioned. Anyone who shows any hesitation about junking time-tested procedures and leaping blindfold into the world of the future is immediately compared to those who refused to rush and buy the first horseless carriages.

It is true that someone had to buy the horseless carriages that led to improvement in the roads, that led to improvement in the horseless carriages. It is open to question, however, whether each individual library is called upon to pioneer in areas where so many experiments are in progress already. Surely it is not unreasonable for a library to say: "Show us a system that is actually doing what we want done, in a situation comparable with ours, and show proof that your proposed new system is better than our present one—and then we'll talk. Don't tell us that no ready-made computer system is fully transplantable into any other situation than the one it was designed for. There are a thousand libraries with problems exactly like ours. We buy standard charging machines, standard furniture, standard typewriters. When you have one or more standard solutions to those problems, tested and debugged, let us know. We can wait."

You will, of course, be told that the system being proposed to you *is* a tested system—that it is in fact being used in such-and-such a library. That may indeed be so, but under no circumstances is it safe to accept secondhand assurances of this, least of all from someone who stands to gain from getting you to jump on the automation band-wagon—whether hardware salesman, software salesman, or consultant. Check up. If the cited example is too far away to visit, bide your time. Wait until the world of the future has beaten its path a bit closer to your door.

You might be told of the automation at the Montclair Public Library. A brochure describing this installation was for twenty years trotted out by IBM representatives as proof that they had something for libraries. Hundreds of librarians visited Montclair to see it. Yet not even the IBM Company ever saw fit to duplicate the equipment that had been custom-made for this application.

Consult Experience of Other Libraries

When you do visit a system represented as having proved out a particular system, you are very likely to find (a) that it is not in fact in actual operation, though they are working on it (find out how long they have been working on it, and how much longer this was than originally projected); (b) that they tried it, but gave it up; (c) that it is operational, but that there have been some difficulties about getting computer time when needed, and the old manual procedures (the elimination of which was the chief justification for the change) are still in use; (d) that it was an "interesting experiment" from which much was learned, but has been "temporarily" set aside; (e) that it is operational and satisfactory, but that cost comparisons between the old way and the new are unavailable; (f) that it is operational and satisfactory and productive of great savings—provided you do not count the cost of the "systems" work, the programming, the conversion, or the computer time (you may be told that the justification for not counting the cost of the computer time is that although the computer time *is being charged* to the library, this is unfair inasmuch as the early justification for the computerization was based on the idea that there was paid for but unused time available on the computer); (g) that the system is a resounding success in every respect, except that the patrons it serves hate it.

You may also, perhaps, find a library system that has successfully solved problems exactly like yours, that has unmistakable proof of resulting gains, that is using a computer exactly like the one available to you, and that is willing to give you (or sell you) a complete set of its procedures manuals, program decks, conversion procedures—and lend you its chief operations manager for a year to train your staff, and supervise the conversion of your procedures. (If you ever hear of a case of this kind, let me know.)

Caution the Watchword

Far and away the best way to computerize is s-l-o-w-l-y. After all, what's the hurry? Computers are steadily coming down in price, and going up in versatility. There may even come a time when the supply of competent programmers begins to catch up to the demand. (If you think it is hard to find and attract qualified librarians, wait until you start looking for computer personnel—in a field where someone with six months experience is considered an old hand, and where standards of accreditation are unknown.)

In the world of business the decision to explore automation is often taken out of competitive considerations: the feeling is that it might be risky to let a competitor get too far ahead. A public library should, presumably, be able to resist this kind of pressure. You are not in competition with other public libraries; and if other libraries choose to blaze the trail, you can reasonably assume that you will have easy access to what they learn.

Eventually, perhaps, it will even be possible to get pretested "software," instead of being on your own from the time they wheel in the hardware. You may never before have bought any device that did not come with some sort of guarantee that it would do the work you bought it to do. Not so with computers. If your programs don't work in the machine you rented, that's your problem. One library wholesaler installed precisely what IBM recommended, only to find that it was woefully inadequate, at which the salesman cheerfully conceded his mistake, and proposed to correct it by bringing in three times the equipment at three times the rental.

When a school publication found its new computer installation completely inadequate to process its September subscription load, the computer company's "experts" apologized and said, "How were we to know that you had to process more subscriptions in September than in any other month?"

Another possible reason for moving slowly is to allow time for examining your library's own automation needs in the context of county or state needs. You ought to be getting your feet wet, but it could be wise to defer any big plunge until you can feel sure it wouldn't lock you out of desirable cooperative ventures a few years ahead, or perhaps deprive you of a chance to share heavy conversion costs with others.

You may well be told: "Gradual conversion is piecemeal conversion. Why computerize the paying of people and not the paying of vendors? Why computerize your purchasing and paying, but not your cataloging? And if the cataloging, why not take the next logical step and abolish your card catalogs and substitute printed book catalogs? And if you computerize your catalog, why not plan for mechanized searching of the catalog? And while you are at it, what about moving farther into automatic ordering plans, to save the time of the book selectors for the more difficult buying decisions?"

Further against gradual conversion it can be argued that massive changes are more likely to succeed than gradual changes. Where backsliding is possible, backsliding must be expected. Most people can do things better at first by old familiar methods, than by new and unfamiliar methods: witness the resistance of hunt-and-peck typists to learning touch typing.

Finally, gradual conversion is theoretically more costly than all-at-once conversion. False paths are taken. Machine operations require parallel payrolls, and duplicate housing. Considering that there is going to be staff unhappiness in any case, isn't it better to get it over with as fast as possible?

But there is also a strong case for gradualism. It gives the staff time to adjust to the new technology—and it can be quite a wrench to accept the idea that invisible magnetic dots on a reel of magtape are going to replace a trusty card file. The library also needs time to develop inside expertise. Why should we assume that a still-wet-be-hind-the-ears graduate of some crash course in computers should be able to pick up what he needs to know about library science any more readily than a librarian should be able to pick up what he needs to know about computer science?

And while gradualism may lead to false starts—at least it keeps the mistakes small. No one ever set up a large plan, either, who didn't later have some second thoughts on how he should have done it.

Impact of Automation on Library Personnel

Easing into automation is probably also best in terms of staff relations. No matter how many pronouncements are made about how nobody is going to lose his job, staff members are going to go right on believing that no computerization plan is going to be considered successful unless the computer displaces enough other salaries to cover its own personnel and rental. Management may be convinced that normal staff turnover will take care of this—but this is cold comfort for those staff members who were not planning to leave, but who see their present work being taken over by the computer. To relieve the fear of the unknown, they need time to get some idea of what they might be doing after re-training.

One of the most common arguments in favor of automation is that it will "save manpower." But it is worth asking whether the project under consideration will save the kind of manpower you most want to save. Are your recruitment problems most acute at the professional level, and the projected staff savings all at the lowest clerical level?

Projected Functions of Automation in the Library

Automation in the library can take many forms ranging from simple bookkeeping to full integration of acquisition, cataloging, serials con-trol, circulation control, and information retrieval. Hardly anybody is in very deep, as yet, but some big dreams are being dreamed.

As might be expected, the problems of automating a payroll or a system for encumbering and paying, being of universal applicability, have had a good deal more study than the problems of automating a library catalog.

One of the most difficult aspects of any automation program is in deciding on which "expert" to rely. It is extremely difficult for the layman to distinguish between degrees of expertise. In this field, more than in most, a little knowledge is a dangerous thing. The tipoff to superficiality of knowledge is usually an insistence that anything is possible, that technologies proven out by the banks, or the airlines, or the stock market are all at the service of your library.

Experts fall into several types. There is the "cloud nine" type, who has never stopped to consider how many transactions per minute it takes to validate the techniques used by the banks, airlines, or Wall Street, who has never priced the rental costs of coaxial cable (who doesn't even know that ordinary phone lines won't carry TV screen images), who hasn't grasped the important distinction between tape storage, disk storage, and core storage. He knows you *can* do anything by computer, but he hasn't stopped to ask whether anyone in his right mind would want to.

Then there is the programmer who has undeniably been earning a living at his trade, but who knows about as much of systems design as a radio assembly line worker knows of electronics. He may have been translating from people-language into computer-language without ever even wondering whether the instructions made sense in terms of the goals.

Then there is the computer-oriented systems analyst. If he's any good, he will be a compulsive problem-solver, and may well spend highly paid time solving problems you don't even want solved, e.g., how to devise computer routines to do small volume chores that could be done quicker by hand. If he's an inspired problem-solver, this may or may not go hand in hand with the knack of keeping costs in mind. His personal motivations also warrant consideration: he wouldn't be human if he didn't put personal income or future prospects ahead of your goals. If you got him by outbidding someone else for his services, you may well lose him by the same route.

No decision to automate should ever be taken except in the context of an overall systems analysis made by someone who is not necessarily committed to any particular approach. This can be important. First, you don't want to set up an automated way of doing what you don't want done anyway—and as a general rule, the automaters will give you what you say you want rather than question it. Second, you don't want to prejudice the answers. Perhaps you should not get a computer just yet, so you don't want a computer-happy consultant who never even considers anything else.

Cost Comparison

All too often, discussion of computerization starts with the observation that the library could get some time on a computer located elsewhere—but imperceptibly moves into consideration of programs that would require the full time of an inside computer, or at least access to an entirely different kind of outside computer. The cost of computer time, either way, bears review.

The rental on a typical small computer tends to start at about $3,000 a month including fairly minimal accessories, and can run up to $10,000 a month with surprising ease, if any considerable amount of versatility is demanded.

Sharing a computer with other agencies can, of course, result in a sharing of these costs; time shared equitably on a comparatively modest computer often works out to about $25 an hour—which is not as far below the rates of commercial service bureaus as it first appears when you remember that you pay for your own mistakes when you pay "inside" rates.

A good question to keep sharply in mind is whether the computer applications under discussion would require communication with the computer during the hours the library is open. If so, then you are probably going to need an in-house computer all your own. If not, then time on an outside computer might suffice.

No discussion of computerization ever goes very far without touching on prospects involving "random access," i.e., the capacity to interrogate the computer at any time, and get an immediate answer.

An attractive possibility, for example, is querying the computer on every charge-out, to find out whether this particular borrower is in arrears. This is possible. But this alone could tie up a small computer, or make substantial demands on a large one, and invoke rental costs of several thousand dollars a month. Is it worth it?

Another attractive possibility is having in random access computer memory the entire information in the card catalog, plus information about books on order. In theory, this data store could be interrogated at will from any desired number of locations, determining instantly whether a desired title is in the system or on order, where located, and whether on loan. However, the cost of such a system—even for a library with only 100,000 titles—could well run $15,000 a month or more—not counting some very impressive start-up and conversion costs. (One of the most sobering moments in exploring computerization ideas is when you find out what the telephone company will charge for hooking in remote terminals, since rental of additional "black boxes" is involved at both ends, in addition to the rentals of the lines. These charges are over and above the computer rentals.)

We have all been told so often that "a computer is only a tool—it can be bent to any use," that it can come as a surprise to learn that a computer suited to the handling of a payroll may be quite unable to handle a book catalog; and that a computer suited to handling a book catalog may be quite unable to handle "random access" inquiries; and that a computer versatile enough to handle all of these things may be altogether too costly to justify itself on the basis of the available workload.

Some of the more common misunderstandings that can creep into discussions of computerization include:

(a) That the programming will be a one-time cost. (Somehow there are always ongoing programming costs, because there are always unforeseen demands on the system.)

(b) That computer rentals, and associated costs will be covered out of salaries saved. (This is *very* unusual. Almost everyone who has computerized will confess, if pressed, that any real savings are as yet unrealized—though still hoped for in the future.)

(c) That the library is being offered a real bargain by way of access to a computer with time to spare. (In reality you are being asked to help bail out someone else whose computer plans are not paying off as anticipated, and who hopes to share his miscalculation with you.)

(d) That you will have "guaranteed access" to the outside computer. (But if things get thrown off schedule by some goof or breakdown, will his payroll stand aside for the processing of yours?)

(e) That processing of data by computer is *ipso facto* cheaper than processing the same data by more prosaic means. (It may easily cost more to process punched cards on a computer than on old-fashioned punched card equipment.)

(f) That work requiring a half-hour of computer time will in fact be done in half an hour. (Somehow work that was going to be processed daily winds up being processed weekly, and work that was going to be processed weekly winds up being processed monthly—and between times you are locked away from even manual access to your data.)

(g) That you are going to get computer help on work that in actual fact is too slight to warrant bothering the computer about— and that by common consent will continue to be handled by hand.

In many libraries, the place to start in any modernization or re-evaluation program is with a quantification, *with unit costs,* of what is being done now. A good discipline, all too seldom invoked, is to insist on a rigorous cross-footing of *units* multiplied by unit costs.

It should be possible to estimate, department by department, and element by element, exactly what the library is delivering to the community in exchange for its budget—how many books circulated, reference questions answered, books acquired, books cataloged and processed, patron-hours spent at the open shelves, staff hours spent in contact with the public, children in attendance at story hours, volumes weeded out of the collection, staff hours spent in the book selection process, square feet of net usable building space devoted to each type of function, cost per square foot of space, cost per dollar of staff salaries in fringe benefits, etc., etc.

People unaccustomed to making such calculations are usually quite certain that it cannot be done. They say, "But every day is different." Or they say, "If I tried to keep track of how I spend my time, I would do little else." Or they say, "All I could give you would be wild guesses."

What they may not realize is: guesses are both acceptable and extremely useful. Furthermore, guesses tend to refine themselves in the very act of doing the guessing. If, for example, a library tries to place a unit value on each element in its operation—does the sum of the units add to the overall outlays? If not, what was forgotten? What elements charged to "general," or "overhead," or "miscellaneous" need further breaking down?

A few lines of inquiry which sometimes prove productive are as follows:

How long does it take us now from the decision to order an available book to the time it goes into use? How is the time spent? To what extent could it be shortened—and how much do we care?

Could a value be placed on the cost of *not* having a book? If, for example, the effective life of an important but topical book were to be taken as six months, but we didn't get it into circulation until a third of that time had passed, could it be said that we had deprived our patrons of a third of the potential value of that book?

Do we have—or need—more than one procedure for ordering books, e.g., an express method for available, topical books, and a more deliberate method for books ordered well in advance of publication, or well in advance of the need? In ordering replacements do we anticipate the need or permit ourselves to be needlessly out of a title we had intended to keep available?

Is there a class of book in our library which is always in circulation, and never on the shelf? Should we buy more duplicate copies of these, so that those patrons who browse and select from what they find will not be deprived of the chance to see occasionally on the shelves the books that the reserve borrowers are cueing up for?

Is there a class of book in our library which never circulates, though purchased with circulation in mind?

Do we have a practical means of informing ourselves about these "never in" or "never out" titles for whatever it might teach us about how to improve our selection procedures? If not, should we seek such a capability in any new approach to circulation control?

Do we know how many people use our various departments except as circulation figures reveal it? Should we know this, or at least spot-check it regularly, in case some re-allocation of space or staff should seem indicated to give the greatest service to the greatest number?

What, precisely, are the reasons for making and filing each piece of paper we handle? Do we know the cost of maintaining each file? The number of times it is used? The cost per use? Does this cost seem justified in every case? Of all the files we keep, which is the one that would be least missed if not kept? (Are all our files up-to-date? If not, is this perhaps presumptive evidence that the ones not being kept up are not really vital?)

Are we perhaps taking certain security measures on a 100 percent basis, when spot-checking might suffice? For example, could we afford to pay on receipt of invoice, without awaiting positive verification of

receipt of books, in reliance on the good faith and ultimate account-
ability for our vendors?

What percentage of our income goes for books? Why is this figure
what it is? (Statistics drawn from the successive editions of the *American Library Directory* show that the average percent of public library
funds going for books has been moving quite steadily upward—but
ranges from 10 percent to 25 percent. British practice puts the figure
higher.)

A major goal of computerizing ordering procedures seems often to
be a foolproof way of encumbering funds. Not all libraries, however,
consider it important to encumber funds on an item-by-item basis.
Some simply ask each branch or department to stay roughly within
assigned budgetary limits—and trust them to do so. After all, how far
overboard could they go? (It is sometimes also possible to put the
burden for not going beyond prescribed limits on the vendor.)

There are some good reasons to study the potentials of automation.
There are also some poor reasons, e.g., that there is idle time on a
computer housed elsewhere; that some computer-happy systems man
elsewhere in the city government wants a computer, and wants you to
help him justify it; that someone somewhere is being called unpro-
gressive and wants to prove he isn't; that the work of a certain
department is in a mess, and "automation" is the first answer that
comes to mind.

Evaluations of the advantages of computerization commonly cheat a
little. Projected costs, based on the assumption that everything has
been foreseen and that nothing will go wrong, are compared with
actual past costs which included the unforeseen. Projected costs
usually assume total abolition of former files and procedures: in an
actual case, a five-part form was to be replaced by a one-part form, but
the five-part form survived also. Projected costs often assume certain
sacrifices, e.g., radical abridgement of the information on the catalog
card, but without exploration of what such abridgement might save
under existing procedures.

Projected advantages place great stress on new capabilities for data
analysis—whether or not these alone would seem worth a very high
price. (The Montclair Public Library had the first punched-card circulation system, highly touted as permitting all kinds of analysis, yet
after the first joyful experimentation with this information gadgetry,
the capability was not even used again for twenty years.)

In the computer field where IBM has the lion's share of the overall business, it nevertheless pays to remember that Univac, and Honeywell, and RCA, and GE, and NCR are all competing successfully—and should definitely be allowed to make proposals, or bid on your "specs." RCA won the contract to automate the card division of the Library of Congress. After close study of the alternatives, Bowker selected a Univac. Many publishers use Honeywell equipment, and at least one changed over from IBM to Honeywell. It is not even inevitable that a library should select the same kind of equipment used elsewhere in the city. Two computers from the same manufacturer are not necessarily compatible with each other, and two computers from different manufacturers are not necessarily *in*compatible with each other.

Is there a computer in your library's future? Undoubtedly. But it is a pity that the words "automation" and "computer" are so often used as if they were synonymous both with each other and with "forward-looking." So much emphasis on the "machine" tends to obscure the fact that machines are only one tool of effective management. In a great many situations a rethinking of procedures that have really had no recent review may well produce fairly important breakthroughs without introduction of any hardware. "If you have always done it that way, it must be wrong." Not only the march of invention, but also changes in salary levels, goals, and attitudes suggest that all procedures of long standing should be required to re-justify themselves from time to time. It is quite literally true that many an unsuccessful computer conversion might well have shown substantial gains—if only they had stopped just short of actually bringing in the computer.

Chapter Seventeen

The Trustee
and Public Relations

BY VIRGINIA H. MATHEWS
AND DAN LACY

P UBLIC RELATIONS is a management function, an instrument of policy and policy makers. In its most significant and highest form, it may be an instrument of institutional development as well as interpretation.

Many people have the mistaken idea that public relations is just the art of making things "look good" or perhaps even better than they are; others think of it simply as the process of tooting your own horn. It is, in fact, not quite either of these. Although publicity and even a kind of press agentry may play a part in carrying out fully a good public relations program, the total program is infinitely more complex. It must start with a concept that includes not only a picture of what the institution is and what it does at present, but a vision of what it could be and what it could do for every individual within range of its pro-

MISS MATHEWS is Deputy Director of the National Library Week Program and Staff Associate of the National Book Committee.

MR. LACY, a trustee of the Irvington-on-Hudson (N.Y.) Public Library, is Senior Vice President of the McGraw-Hill Book Company.

gram and services. Most importantly, a good public relations program must convey how an institution relates to the wider concerns of the community.

Importance of Public Relations to the Library

An on-going, comprehensive, and high-level public relations and public information program is a necessity for every public library and library system, no matter what its size, that wants to make the difficult transition from being, for most of the public, a fringe benefit to being of central economic and social importance to the wide cross-section of people of all classes and economic levels.

The public library has turned in a few short years from being an agency aloof from the political process and supported by a sort of refined annual-giving on the part of the community into a contender, with other basic public services, for an appropriate share of the tax dollar. What the community, and the state and the nation, believe to be an "appropriate share" will depend in large part on how good a job of "public relating," or relating the library to the public, has been done by each library and the cumulative impact of this effort.

The Trustee's Responsibility Toward Public Relations

Much of the library's day-to-day public relations is carried out, of course, by the staff, but it is the trustees who represent the library and all it stands for to responsible leader-colleagues in all areas of community life and concern. Library trustees should have a wide background of civic and cultural interests in the community, giving them contacts among various groups and organizations and unlimited opportunities to "talk library" to friends, fellow members, and business associates. Just as the library staff has the duty of maintaining good services and good relations with all members of the public, so is the trustee under obligation to act as library ambassador in all community contacts, turning such contacts into channels for building respect and a sense of commitment toward the library and all it stands for.

Library board members, therefore, must understand not only what services the library offers but how these services can be useful, for example, to businessmen, young mothers with preschool children, high school dropouts, and welfare clients. Further, they must know what programs and services the library does not offer and why. Beyond this, the library board member must be able to convey how the very existence of a good library affects the climate of the community as the library provides balance and depth-resources to the mass media while supporting intellectual freedom and the right of the individual to form his own judgment and listen for the sound of his own drummer. To reflect his own library's purpose and goals intelligently, the trustee must know not only its policies and programs but how it compares with libraries in similar community circumstances; he must have a sense of his library's place in a nationwide system of libraries of all types.

One most important responsibility of the library board and each of its trustees is that of diplomatic and political relations with governing authorities. A cornerstone of these relations is the annual report of the library board. The board, together with the librarian, should make certain that an interesting, comprehensive report is published and widely distributed and publicized. This report, in addition to summarizing operational facts, new programs, and such, should cover needed changes that will keep the library not only abreast of but hopefully one jump ahead of growth and change in the community.

The Public to be Reached

In thinking about other specifics of a public relations program, these questions must be asked: what sort of relations and what public? The first question is relatively easy to answer: the library wants a relationship of *use* with the public. It is poor practice to think of a public relations program as an isolated special project to gain support for a new building or a jump in the budget. Considered in this light, it will be a failure. Libraries exist for the purpose of serving, not for the purpose of being supported. The proper aim of the public relations program is to enlarge that service. If this is well done, the library will have gone most of the way toward solving the problem of support. Of course, the people of the community may understand library needs, but nothing that can be said of them will have any meaning unless people have first experienced its services.

The second question is, what is the public to which the library needs to be related? The answer to this one is the public that is not now using, or making adequate use of, the library. In most communities this unserved public is far larger than today's hordes of student users may lead one to suppose. Bernard Berelson's important book, *The Library's Public,* estimates that in the typical American municipality only a minority of the adult population use the public library at all and only a very small minority, indeed, use it regularly. Tremendous social changes in the two decades since the publication of this study have wrought tremendous and sweeping changes in library use, but all current estimates indicate that regular adult users are still far in the minority in a total population of over 200 million. The explosions of population and of knowledge, the transformation of our educational system at all levels, the communications revolution, and the rising aspirations of the underclass have changed the make-up and the needs of the library's public, in effect splintering it into many different and much more demanding publics. The use of the library for light recreational reading, predominant at the time of Berelson's study, has all but vanished; purposeful use of library resources in relation to social and economic growth and development is the order of the day.

As the library has come to serve more kinds of needs for more varieties of publics, its role in the community has vastly expanded. The basic role of the public relations program is to keep on reaching out to more and more citizens, to seek out those who do not yet use the library, and to relate the library to them. It must reach out to people in terms of the imperatives of our social upheaval, of individual uncertainty, in terms of each individual's needs and interests. No longer is it enough just to be there for those who wish to come. The library now has to undertake the infinitely more difficult task of responding to needs not yet fully realized, of first stimulating the interests it will later hope to satisfy.

Where is this great majority of the public who are not library users? By definition, they are not in the library. Most are probably not enthralled by reading for its own sake, nor interested in books per se (although many habitual readers supply many of their needs by buying paperback books, which have the virtue of being accessible and disposable). They do not read a review column on new books in the newspaper; an exhibit of books in the library will not reach them. This kind of publicity is useful and even essential, but it addresses itself, basically, to the small minority of citizens who are traditional and assured library users, rather than serving to make the library relevant to a new segment of the public.

Essential Specifics to Consider

What are some of the specifics that should be considered for doing this job?

1. Remember that most nonusers of the library are not people who get great pleasure from reading itself. Reading, if they do it at all and with any ease, is a means not an end. With practice, experience, and ready access to books most people can come to derive real satisfaction and enjoyment from reading. But there is no man, woman, or child, reader or nonreader, who does not have needs which the library can help him meet. He must be sought in terms of those needs. Even the reader who supplies himself with books from nonlibrary sources may learn to use the library for other media, for information or research.

2. Until very recently publicity and promotion efforts for libraries were thought of as an attempt to "get people into the library." Now we recognize that the important thing is to interest people in using some library resources and services, even if they never come into the main library at all. An important part of the library's public relations program still needs to be addressed to appropriating bodies and those who fix budgets, to help them understand that mere circulation is no longer a valid budgeting base for an institution with the social and economic responsibilities of today's public library.

3. Remember Tom Sawyer—let others whitewash the library fence. One of the splendid and satisfying experiences of the past decade, with its burgeoning awareness of the value of libraries and the development of real financial support for their work, has been the demonstration, over and over again, that leaders in all professions and all the communications media, and citizens in every walk of life—from the largest city to the smallest village—all are eager to help interest others in using and supporting libraries. The intellect and the qualities of independent thought that are served by books, by reading, and by libraries are these days increasingly valued as social organization and technology become more and more complex and individuation more precious and difficult of achievement. There will be more than willingness; there will be eagerness and anxiety to strengthen libraries and their resources.

4. When the library does seek community support for its growing services, the board must plan well, have clear goals that people can

understand, and be bold. Little plans, inadequate budgets, partial service, awaken no enthusiasm, challenge no friends to action. There is no dollar a community invests more thriftily than the dollar it puts to work nourishing the minds and spirits of its adults and its youth through their library. Every member of the library board must believe this if he is to be an effective trustee. The board must first dream the library the community really ought to have, then lay those dreams before the community in clear terms. Let friends—all the friends of the library and of the board—help, and if the library and board have served the community well, the response will be beyond one's fondest hopes. The library board holds in trust one of the community's most intimate, most influential services; it is the trustees' responsibility to demand the best for it.

The National Library Week Program: A Public Relations Process

The National Library Week Program offers a special opportunity to library trustees. It offers a time to start, a time to evaluate, an occasion and reason for making new approaches to people, to organizations, to other agencies, to problems, and to opportunities. Herein lies its "year-roundness" despite the paradox of its name. Trustees and librarians who think of the Program as a *process* to use, rather than something to be done, will get full value from it. It is the learning by lay public, trustees, and librarians that goes on while preparing for the April week of national impact that yields the big and long-range rewards: the new understanding and commitment to library goals, the new contacts, the new users.

The National Library Week Program was launched in 1958. It developed out of the strong conviction of its sponsors that reading is an important source of personal fulfillment; that only by making possible the intellectual development of every individual to the limits of his capacity will the national interest best be served; and that libraries of all kinds, as the means of making reading materials and information readily accessible to all people who need them, should be used fully and supported properly. Sponsored by the National Book Committee, Inc., a nonprofit, educational membership organization, in cooperation with the American Library Association, NLW is now an established continuing program; its purpose remains to encourage lifetime reading habits, to increase the use of libraries of all types, and to expand the total reading and library resources of the nation.

The tremendous public response to the Program from its first year is evidence of widespread belief in its objectives and a general concern for the quality of intellectual life in the community and the nation. Thousands of librarians, publishers, newspaper editors, broadcasters, civic and education groups, and business, religious, and professional leaders have devoted their time, skills, and money to reminding Americans that the freedom to read is the privilege and responsibility of citizens of a free democratic society. In April of each year the week itself, as distinct from the year-round program bearing its name, is both the climax and the starting point of many year-round activities that spur Americans to read more themselves and to accept the responsibility for making reading opportunities more readily available to others.

Need for an Organized National Program

Why is such a program needed? Because, as library trustees are well aware, the great majority of people read very little or not at all. They may lack the motivation, the ability, the opportunity, or all three. Yet every major social, educational, and economic development in our country today is tending vastly to increase the nation's need for better readers and for greatly improved library services and facilities. Among these demanding changes are an exploding population; an expanding body of knowledge that needs to be made readily available to an increasing number of people; the trend in education at all levels toward greater reliance on research and individual work by the student; the need for job flexibility and retraining to meet the needs of a constantly shifting economy; and an increase in leisure time, resulting from a shorter work week and earlier retirement.

The growth of library facilities in recent years is encouraging, but the need has grown even faster. Millions of people still have no library service; millions more have only poor service. Fully one-half of the elementary schools—the level at which talent can most easily be fostered and reading and study habits formed—have no libraries. Many high school and college libraries are grossly inadequate now and within the decade must provide for additional millions of students.

Only widespread public understanding of these facts and their significance will bring about support for the drastic improvements necessary. Librarians working alone or with a handful of faithful trustees and other lay helpers cannot do the job. The NLW Program should be regarded as a prime opportunity for reaching as many people as possible with the message that libraries of all types—school, college, and public—must be centrally involved in helping to solve some of the burning problems of our time. NLW must encompass nationally a two-pronged message: an appeal to the readers, the civic-minded, the socially, politically, and economically responsible; and a warm invitation to the nonreader and those unaware of their need or of the existing means of satisfying it.

The Trustee's Role in NLW

At the ALA Conference in Montreal in 1960 the American Library Trustee Association adopted the following statement of policy:

> Whereas, the public library trustees in each community have the basic responsibility for providing the best possible library service to its citizens of all ages;
> Be it therefore resolved that trustees should use National Library Week as a time to spotlight the needs and services of all the library resources in the community and to enlist the support of citizens' groups in a year-round program; and
> The American Library Trustee Association recommends that trustees take the lead in forming local community NLW committees composed of civic, educational, cultural, and recreational leaders to promote better library services.

Recognizing the special tasks imposed by legal authority and responsibility for the development of public libraries that reside in public library trustees, it is nonetheless important that trustees learn to think earnestly also of their larger responsibility as leaders for total library development in the community. A basic tenet of the NLW Program is that it be concerned with all types of libraries required to provide total library service to all the people of a community. The point in time has been reached when everyone concerned with libraries, whatever his special orientation to a type of library, must learn to think in terms of total library development for the community, the state, and the nation. It is no longer possible for one type of library facility in the community to forge ahead in splendid insularity; library publics have merged and surged and shifted across jurisdictional lines, and are coming to expect all libraries to serve them and serve them well whenever they are needed.

In most cases trustees are the only officials appointed or elected to serve the community by concerning themselves solely with library matters. The NLW Program is the ideal vehicle for activating and implementing this concern. On two counts—that of official responsibility and that of broad philosophical leadership—trustees are of central importance to the planning and development of the NLW Program and its ultimate effectiveness. If the effort is to succeed, it must have the wholehearted support of the library board as a body and the individual help of all its members throughout the program.

Since the NLW Program is essentially a public information and implementation program geared to the achievement of objectives, it is most important that the objectives be defined right from the start. Publicity and program activities are only the final steps in the planning of a public relations program; it must start with development of the concept that is to be conveyed.

Planning State and Local NLW Programs

The entire planning process for NLW Programs can be summarized somewhat as follows:

1. *Define Policies*

Be able to convey succinctly what good library service is (in all types of libraries) and why it is essential to individuals, the community, the state, and the nation.

2. *Mobilize Facts*

Be able to state briefly *where we are*—the facts about the present level of library services and facilities.

3. *Compare*

What is with *what needs to be* in order to satisfy present and future demands for library services. The difference between them constitutes the existing gap between present facilities and services and good library service.

4. *Identify Goals*

Short-term, intermediate, and long-range. These are the steps which, taken in sequence, will lead to achievement of ultimate objectives.

5. *Blocks to Goals*

Recognize factors that stand in the way of goal achievement, and map a plan for overcoming them. Blocks may take the form of an inadequate tax base, library laws that require revision, public apathy, and limited vision as to what good libraries can do for people, or individuals who are blocking progress.

6. *Involve and Inform*

The leadership echelon in the state and community must be involved and informed so that they may involve and inform others. These are the people who make up the power structure; they are the people who have channels to and influence with various publics; they are those who are willing and able to shoulder a share of public responsibility and through whom and by whom things get done.

7. *Disseminate*

The "what," the "why," the "where we are," and what needs to be done about it, and how to go about it through programs and publicity.

The opportunity to awaken and sustain interest, concern, and enthusiasm for library development in people with the ability to help bring it about is one of the most important values NLW offers. Without an active, strong local committee made up of top leadership in all fields, the full potential of NLW cannot be realized. Remember that National Library Week is not an end in itself, nor is it really a week. It is primarily a reason for an opportunity to involve lay leadership in library development—a whole widened circle of powerful new allies.

The local committee should include the public librarian and a library trustee, one or more school librarians, a college or university librarian in the community, and any special librarian who may serve local industry or an institution. This nucleus professional group expands into a full committee with the addition of laymen, and it continues to provide guidance to the lay members in planning the program. The essential element is the conviction and background knowledge of the librarians and trustees, conveyed first to other members of the committee and thence outward to the community.

Importance of Goals

Short-term, intermediate, and long-range goals, serving as sequential steps toward a full range of good library services, are important. Goals which might be short-term or intermediate for one community may be long-range goals for another. Some goals form stepping stones to others. A few suggested examples might be:

1. Establishment of a continuing committee of citizen leaders to work year-round on development of better library service. Many such groups have grown out of NLW committees.

2. Communication with municipal, county, and state officials regarding new or revised legislation permitting development of libraries, or if such legislation is already pending, mobilization of support for it.

3. Support of cooperation in a regional system, informing officials and the public of the advantages of participation.

4. Building of support in advance for future bond issues, larger tax appropriations, new building, bookmobile service, etc., by acquainting taxpayers and public officials with library needs.

5. Cooperation with the school board, administrators, teachers, parents, and the public in a school library program.

6. Cooperation with college boards, administrators, and alumni groups in planning adequate library service for all colleges in the community.

7. Working out a closer relationship between adult education agencies, study groups, and all civic and service organizations of the community with the library.

8. Close cooperation with youth-serving agencies, vocational guidance people, and other youth leaders in encouragement of reading as an important part of their continuing programs.

9. Encouragement of librarianship as a career, through school and other youth-guidance channels.

10. Interesting local newspapers, bulletins, and house organs in carrying regular book reviews; initiation of a regular book review or library-oriented program on local radio or TV stations.

Trustee-Oriented Special Activities

Numerous special activity suggestions and specific advice about newspaper, radio, and TV publicity are given in the National Library Week *Local Organization Handbook*. The most recent edition is available from NLW headquarters at One Park Avenue, in New York City. The following are some general procedural suggestions, with some examples of categories of activities that might prove useful:

1. The board should officially endorse the NLW Program and the formation of a local NLW committee, and be represented on the committee by at least one of its members.

2. Trustees should be aware of NLW as an opportunity to transform the community into a *reading* community, in the understanding that use and support of the library will increase only when the whole climate of intellectual interest and education is improved.

3. Trustees should provide leadership to the committee in "thinking big." Bold plans often succeed where timid proposals fail. The supporters of libraries, present and potential, will work harder for a major improvement than for token improvements.

4. The board can help to ensure enlistment of an influential citizen (nontrustee) as chairman of the committee and suggest individuals and organizations for active roles in the campaign. Trustees are the natural link between library interests and other influential people in the community.

5. Well in advance of the organization of the local NLW committee, the library board should prepare itself to serve as a source of facts, figures, and development philosophy, with a view to providing guidance to the committee in formulating and implementing goals. For examples, trustees might:

> Undertake an informal evaluative study of the present program of public library services and outline their development objectives in relation to the growing or changing needs of the community.
>
> Institute a survey of the library's program by an outside authority (consultant from the state library, for example) so that specific recom-

mendations and objectives may be ready for implementation by the local committee.

Start a continuing project of study of ALA Standards for public libraries. At each board meeting one member might give a report on one section of the Standards, followed by discussion that relates them to the local situation.

Familiarize themselves especially with methods of extending service, such as branches, bookmobiles, and possibilities for instituting cooperative ventures with other libraries and community service agencies in the area.

As a special project in aid of the committee, make a study of library legislation or revision of library laws, at the state and local level, needed to achieve a system of cooperative development on a county, regional, or other area basis. Findings should be presented to the local committee as a basis for appropriate action to gain support for such measures through the NLW Program.

Prepare for NLW use a program of color slides showing deficiencies and potentialities for library service in the community.

6. Each board of trustees is urged to undertake the following special project: to send, during National Library Week, a packet of facts and information about their library and its services to concerned government officials at all levels—the mayor, councilmen, representatives, and others. Avoid lengthy reports that may not be read or absorbed. Organize the essential facts for a simple, clear-cut presentation: *what is, what should be,* and *why it is important* to the people of the community that these needs be met.

7. Trustees as a group, and working in concert with the local committee, might make NLW the occasion for other special projects:

Offer their services, individually and as a body, for NLW activities: as a speaker's bureau, as hosts at coffee hours or at a series of open houses for specific community groups.

Visit libraries in other communities (of similar size) known to have superior library service; be prepared to make comparisons in "NLW talks."

Launch a drive, during the "Week," to encourage appropriate gifts and memorials to the library by organizations and individuals, to urge establishment of special collections and services.

Contact and urge lawyers to suggest consideration of the library as a beneficiary when wills are drawn.

Emphasize to business leaders the important role of the library in attracting new industry to the area. Modern plant location surveys generally stress data on education and cultural resources, as well as economic advantages. (In one state trustees in several towns scheduled meetings with committees of the state's economic council to discuss necessary library improvements.)

8. Trustees should use the NLW Program as an opportunity to become acquainted with the function of school libraries and the status of their development in the community's schools. They should explore with the school board and administration, who are financially responsible for school library development, the ways in which the public and school library can work cooperatively.

9. Trustees should encourage NLW activity with built-in follow-up: organization, or reactivation, of a "Friends" group; establishment of a year-round program for the NLW citizens' committee. Trustees can help to ensure that such a group plays a focal continuing role in working toward the achievement of development goals.

10. A local board of trustees might urge or inaugurate a regional or even statewide trustee workshop which would include consideration of the ways that trustees can work more effectively with local NLW committees.

Basic Purpose of NLW

The NLW Program approaches the task of awakening understanding by trying to do three basic things: inspire, inform, and involve. People must first be aroused and made aware of their need for reading, for information, for continuing self-education. They must be encouraged to believe that what they learn and think and contribute has meaning not only for themselves but for their community and their nation. Along with this, they must be informed that libraries can and should be able to offer them a range of knowledge and enjoyment to satisfy every interest and purpose. Finally, they must become involved; encouraged to make fuller use of existing library facilities, demand more of them, and take action to improve them.

To do these things, NLW operates in different ways at the national, state, and local community levels. A national framework of broad concepts attracts public attention; at the state level these concepts are related to the opportunities and needs of the people in each particular state. It remains for the NLW committee in each local community to focus the general awareness on the reading and library resources of that community. It is here that specific information and concrete action can bring libraries and potential readers together and result in demand and support for better libraries.

Chapter Eighteen

The Trustee
and Censorship

BY ALEX ALLAIN

AND ERVIN GAINES

> ". . . free men and
> free inquiry are
> inseparable."[1]

Aᴌᴍᴏsᴛ ᴅᴀɪʟʏ, somewhere in the United States, libraries
are confronted by the problem of self-appointed censors. Right wingers
object to "liberal" books; liberals object to books which promote "un-
enlightened attitudes"; religious people of all denominations object
to books which they feel misrepresent their religion or their ethical
values; patriots object to books which suggest that the American system could use some improvement; and, worst of all, puritanical people
object to books which, in their view, corrupt the morals of the community. Any librarian with a few years' experience could expand the
list *ad infinitum,* recalling with shudders particular instances of well-

[1] Former President Johnson, commenting on Edward R. Murrow's beliefs.

MR. ALLAIN is a trustee of the St. Mary Parish (La.) Library and a member
of the ALA Intellectual Freedom Committee.

MR. GAINES is the Director of the Minneapolis Public Library and Past Chairman of the ALA Intellectual Freedom Committee.

meaning censors indignantly demanding the removal of dirty, defamatory, sacrilegious, or un-American books from the shelves.

Librarians, of course, are the most directly involved in this dreary task of facing self-appointed censors. They are the ones who bear the brunt of the attacks, hear the insults, and, should the censor be indignant enough, face legal action. But trustees are involved just as deeply, even if less directly. For they are the ones who are responsible for selecting the librarian in the first place, then for setting the policy under which the library operates.

The Board's Responsibility: Book Selection Policy

Primary among the policies the trustees must set is the one governing book selection. This policy must be enunciated before book selection begins, for a board without policy, and therefore a library without a policy, can be compared to a ship without a rudder. It is too late to formulate policies when an attack comes. Then confusion and chaos prevail with everyone shifting the blame to someone else, and eventually the public is left shorn of its freedom to read. Therefore, the policy governing book selection should be set firmly by the trustees, and it should be reaffirmed by succeeding boards, to insure both that the policy remains timely and that all incoming board members are knowledgeable about the policy and agree to it.

Trustees must recognize, in setting policy, that American communities are made of people of varied backgrounds, interests, religions, ethnic groups, educational levels, and that, as far as possible, the books selected should reflect this variety. American communities are composed of people holding conflicting ideas or wondering which of two opposite views they should adopt. The books selected should, as much as possible, reflect those conflicting opinions and present these opposite points of views so that the reading public will have a chance to reach its own conclusions, even if those conclusions are not the ones held by librarians or by the trustees.

As John Stuart Mill stated eloquently, only our willingness to have our beliefs, however cherished, challenged, gives us the right to hold them and act upon them: "The beliefs which we have most warrant for, have no safeguard to rest on, but a standing invitation to the world to prove them unfounded. If the challenge is not accepted, or is accepted and the attempt fails, we are far enough from certainty still; but we have done the best that the existing state of human reason admits of; we have neglected nothing that could give the truth a chance of reaching us. . . . This is the amount of certainty attainable by fallible being, and this the sole way of attaining it."

The Librarian's Responsibility: Book Selection

The policy for book selection must be set by the trustees, but the daily work of selection must be vested in the librarian and the other professional staff members who are qualified by reason of education and training. Any book or library material so selected should be held to be selected by the board. By the very nature and definition of their roles, the trustees represent the public who own the library; they are charged with multiple responsibilities, the two most important being the employment of a competent and qualified librarian and the adoption of written policy to govern the operation and program of the library. The librarian is charged with the administration of the library under the policies set by the board. The duties and responsibilities of the board do not overlap those of the librarian. Book selection within the framework of the policy is an administrative function and is one of the duties and responsibilities of the librarian.

It is obvious that the librarian should carry out the actual selections. Librarians are professionals, trained in making a balanced selection for library shelves; they keep up with new books through professional journals and book reviews sections and, despite the usual jokes about librarians never reading anything besides the blurb on the dust jacket, try to keep up with at least the more important new publications. They are therefore, because of their training and because of the very nature of their job, the best qualified to select books.

Some libraries, unfortunately, are too small or too impoverished to have the services of a librarian. When this happens the makers of policy should not assume the administrative function of book selection. If such staff as is available cannot assume this duty, the advice of the state library should be sought.

The Board Must Support the Librarian

Once the trustees have chosen a librarian and stated the book selection policy to be followed, they must be prepared to follow through and accept their share of the abuse which may be heaped upon the hapless librarian. They must make it clear, both to the librarian and to the public, that books selected by the librarian are considered to have been selected by the board. If they do not think the librarian competent enough to have that much authority delegated, they should look for another one. The total and unconditional support of the librarian by the trustees is the best means of preserving the freedom to read for all Americans.

Books or other library material should be selected on the basis of their value of interest, information, and enlightenment of all people of the community. No book or library material should be excluded because of the race or nationality of the author or because of his political or social views. It must be absolutely clear that censorship is a purely individual matter, and that while anyone is free to reject for himself books which he does not approve of, he must not and should not be allowed to exercise censorship to restrict the free choice of others.

Book Selection Must Reflect a Variety of Opinions

The books selected should not reflect the political, religious, or moral biases of either the librarian or the trustees. They should, on the contrary, reflect the variety of opinion available in a free society. There are times when this objective criterion might be neither easy nor pleasant for either the librarian or trustees. A liberal might well cringe at seeing the library carry *Race and Reason;* a conservative might shudder at encountering a copy of *The Cause Is Mankind.* It is not pleasant for a Catholic librarian to order Blanshard's works, nor for a liberal to purchase the books of Goldwater or Buckley. A Catholic librarian should not use the *Index* as a guide for this collection. Neither should a staunch Protestant eliminate a book merely because it bears a bishop's *imprimatur.* The public library, built, operated, and financed to serve the public must present all points of views. Internal censorship, whether it arises from the biases of the librarian or from the fear of public outcry, is as dangerous for the freedom to read as the external censorship of well-meaning fanatics.

"Pornography" on the Library Shelves?

"Pornography," whatever it is, is of course a main target in censorship. There again, neither the taste of the librarian nor that of the trustee should determine the selection. Librarians and the trustees might well agree with most reviewers that John Updike's *Couples* is a tasteless, boring, unimaginative story of wifeswapping, more suitable for the jokes told by the boys in the backroom than for library shelves. Yet if the public wants to read it, and the waiting list in most public libraries indicates that it does, the library should provide it. Nothing, however, forbids librarians and trustees offering prayers for the improvement of public taste.

Before reviling a new book as filthy and worthless, however, librarians and trustees should pause a moment and reflect that the dirty books of one generation often become the classics of the next one and are assigned in college courses and read with as much boredom as other classics. *Tess of the D'Ubervilles, Ulysses, Catcher in the Rye* were all condemned as "dirty" before being included in most standard reading lists. Public librarians and trustees might also do well to look into some of the "classics," and find how frank is the language of Chaucer, Shakespeare, John Donne, or the Bible, to cite just a few. And they might ponder the moral subversion implied in the plays of Euripides or some of the dialogues of Plato. Classics become classics because they say something, and it is impossible to say anything without giving offense to someone.

Freedom to Read Is the Public's Right

The policy should make clear the determination of the board to defend the principles of the freedom to read. The trustees can accomplish this aim by stating that the responsibility for removal of any book from library shelves shall rest only with a court of competent jurisdiction. The freedom to read has been won at high cost. Our people have gone to jail for it, paid heavy fines for it, suffered ostracism for it. The cost has been too great in human effort to allow this essential freedom to be lost inch by inch, by gradual erosion, by small compromises here and there intended to pacify an angry patron or an aroused interest group, or worse, by default or apathy. Every time a librarian gives way and removes a book as objectionable, freedom is eroded. Every time a board of trustees fails to support the librarian's decision, freedom is also eroded.

The selection policy should be set by the trustees firmly and clearly long before they encounter their first self-appointed censor. Both the librarian and trustees should know the arguments before they are presented by the censor. They should also know the answers. They should be able to defend their ground, and, especially, they should be ready to go all the way with their librarian to defend the freedom to read even to the point of fighting the case in court if that is the only way. They must sometimes be ready to suffer abuse, for the censor is often sincere, fanatical, and so thoroughly convinced of his own righteousness that he sees every opponent as a public enemy.

Fortunately, most would-be censors stop as soon as their bluff is called. Finding themselves faced with a self-assured librarian, self-assured because the backing of the trustees is beyond question, most of them will desist. A few more determined ones will want to carry the matter before the board. There again, trustees who have a firmly set policy to present and arguments to back that policy, will usually be able to silence the critic. Whether or not trustees can avoid a confrontation, they can be assured that in a showdown they will prevail. Court decisions over the last few years have tended toward greater leniency in defining "pornography" and have consistently upheld the freedom to read, just as library trustees must, as part of the great freedoms guaranteed by the Bill of Rights of the United States Constitution: the Freedom of Speech and the Freedom of the Press.

Trustees should also be aware of the major principles enunciated by librarians in two documents, The Library Bill of Rights, and The Freedom to Read Statement, both of which will be found in an appendix to this volume.

Chapter Nineteen

Trustees and the Friends of the Library

BY CAY MORTENSON

AND SARAH L. WALLACE

. . . to create public interest in the . . . library and its branches, . . . to promote increased knowledge of its service and needs; and to foster public support for the necessary development of said library to the end that it may serve adequately the needs of the steadily increasing population of . . . the city.[1]

. . . to foster closer relations between the . . . library and the citizens . . . ; to promote knowledge of the functions, resources, services and needs of the library; to lead in the development of a program for the extension and improvement of the library services and resources; and to aid in the provision of adequate housing and other facilities for the library.[2]

. . . to maintain an organization of persons interested in books; to assist in bringing to the library . . . funds for special needs beyond the command of the library budget; to encourage gifts of books and manuscripts; and to cooperate with the librarian and the library advisory board in the development of the resources of the library under the direction of the library committee of the Board of Trustees . . .[3]

[1] Charter of the Friends of the Jacksonville (Florida) Public Library, Inc.
[2] Constitution and Bylaws, Concord (California) Library League.
[3] Constitution of the Associated Friends of the Library of Rutgers University.

MRS. MORTENSON is President of the California Library Trustee Association and has served as Chairman of ALA Friends of Libraries Committee.
MISS WALLACE is Publications Officer, Library of Congress.

Friends of the Library groups, since their beginning in the Midwest in the 1930s, have spread with increasing momentum throughout the United States until they now number in the thousands and have a recognized place in the program of countless public, private, school, college, and university libraries. Quotes such as those which open this chapter, taken from the constitution and bylaws of widely varying groups of Friends of the Library, show more clearly than pages of print the general motivation of the organization of all such groups. Since libraries themselves are highly individual, their Friends will be individual in type and in purpose. Yet, as these quotations demonstrate, there are certain considerations common to all.

Suggestions on how to organize a group of Friends of the Library are available from many sources. (See Appendix IX) The important thing—to the trustees, to the library, and to the future of the Friends themselves—is to start right.

Except for Friends groups formed for the purpose of establishing a library where one does not exist, the new groups should be given the blessing and help of the board members, the librarian, and the staff. If the trustees and the librarian establish an early understanding with the new Friends group regarding its place in the library's overall structure, later jurisdictional problems are less likely to develop. The possibility of misunderstandings developing between Friends and trustees or Friends and librarians can be avoided by ascertaining that the general area of Friends activities and functions be clearly defined at the outset. One Friends group wrote the following formula into its bylaws: "We do not usurp the trustees' prerogatives in establishing policies, nor do we interfere with the library's operating procedures, but we stand back of both."

Friends of any library are interested in a closer relationship between their library and the public it serves. They adopt as one of their goals the promotion of wider knowledge and use of the library and its services. Friends hope to improve those services and to aid in the development of a broader and better program. To accomplish this they also assist in providing the necessary funds to make that program possible whether it be through bond issues for adequate buildings, campaigns for bigger budgets, and for gifts to augment the collection or to add to the equipment of specialized areas such as the audiovisual department, children's room, hospital service, or work with the blind.

Of interest to trustees is the fact that almost without exception these groups recognize their relationship to the librarian and to the library board, pledging themselves in many instances to seek direction from the librarian and the trustees and to structure their program so that it may support the overall framework of the board's plans.

As two librarians of long experience have said: "Organizing and enlisting the help of a large organized auxiliary group of friendly influential men and women has had notable results in spreading public knowledge of the library, enlisting support, getting funds, and passing bond issues. One wonders why it is not almost universal. Some trustees fear that the 'Friends' will get so influential and active that they will tell the trustees how to run the library. A good board should be big-minded enough to work with and welcome ideas from outside."[4]

Friends of the Library who think in terms of community development are almost certain to accomplish more than those who concern themselves solely with library development. The library is not an end in itself; it is the means to an end. It must justify its existence by what it does to increase the community's mental wealth.

One unusually successful group set down these four purposes:

1. To assist every individual and organization in the community concerned with increasing the community's cultural content
2. To explore ways to make more effective use of the present inadequate library and its equipment
3. To materialize the dream of a modern library building, adequately staffed and adequately equipped
4. To make the library the center of a county or area library system

The citizens of the community in which this group originated were not anti-library but merely apathetic, like so many citizens of other communities. Their library had been built with Carnegie funds in 1915. Not an inch had been added to its size in 40 years. The task of creating a desire for a modern library was one beset with difficulties.

The Friends, who had not succumbed to the prevailing apathy, were instrumental in persuading the city to appropriate money for an addition to the old library. A campaign conducted by the Friends raised funds for furnishings. Private gifts bought equipment. The Junior League was persuaded to give a bookmobile which served for eleven years. The bequest of a Friend—$9,000 in government bonds—was

[4] Joseph L. Wheeler and Herbert Goldhor. *Practical Administration of Public Libraries.* Harper and Row, New York and Evanston, 1962, p. 151.

used to create a garden that has served thousands as an outdoor reading room. Another legacy enabled the Friends to widen and screen porches that provided additional reading space. The Friends induced the city council to buy an eight-acre plot in the center of the city upon which to build a modern library. Five years later a million-dollar library was built on that site.

Thus, in 15 years, this group realized a four-point program which might have staggered a larger but less imaginative organization.

Set down in print, the objectives of many groups of Friends seem impossible to the uninitiated. Yet day after day, in large and small communities, their objectives are becoming realities.

Friends of the Library, animated by a definite purpose, intent on giving service, frequently discover that what they need comes to them out of the unknown. Money, assistance, and materials become available, but often people from whom gifts might be expected give nothing but people from whom nothing is expected give with astounding generosity.

It is axiomatic that "if you want people to give, you must ask them for what you want." Citizens cannot possibly know what a library needs unless they are told, over and over, what those needs are. It must be made clear that Friends are fellow citizens who believe that a community is a better community if it has an adequate library.

Each group selects its own objectives. Local needs and resources must dictate conditions. Among the many ways Friends can help are these:

> Improve existing services, buildings, resources, and facilities.
>
> Develop public understanding of libraries and their vital role in today's living.
>
> Stimulate bequests, endowments, and gifts of books, records, films, and other materials, equipment, and money.
>
> Sponsor speakers, book reviews, book fairs, film programs, and other cultural activities.
>
> Arrange fund raising events.
>
> Encourage interest in librarianship as a career through publicity and scholarships.
>
> Aid staff development through funding institutes, in-service programs and opportunities for advanced study.

Friends can make the difference between a mediocre and an outstanding library.

Organization of a Group of Friends

In setting up a group of Friends a great number of members is not the first need. A large membership is desirable; it may provide more adequate funds. However, the real essential is members who have a deep concern for library betterment. Progress is usually the result of the efforts of a comparatively small number of men and women imbued with a high degree of creativity. Given an opportunity to express themselves freely, unhampered by too much organization or too many rules, they can achieve great things.

Practical helps in organizing a group can be found in the experience of others. Professional literature contains such accounts. The Friends of Libraries kit prepared by the Friends of Libraries Committee, Public Relations Section of the Library Administration Division, American Library Association, is another helpful resource.[5]

A typical plan of organization, used successfully by Friends of California Libraries, is seen in Appendix IX.

Friends, Trustees, and the Library Administration

Several times in this chapter it has been pointed out that libraries, and therefore, their Friends, are individual, that their needs and their procedures are based on individual considerations. In referring to the relationship between Friends, trustees, and the librarian this is especially true. Some board members are elected, others are appointed; the latter receive their appointments in a variety of ways from a variety of bodies—city managers, mayors, city councils, judges, courts, school boards, or a combination of several such agencies.

Boards are usually either advisory or policy making; in a comparatively few instances they are administrative. Some libraries have no boards, and when this is the case the Friends have sometimes assumed the role of advisory trustees.

Recognizing such exceptions, this section will confine itself to the more usual situation in which is found the trustees, a library administrator, and a group of Friends. Generally, the trustees come into being

[5] Eugenie M. Suter, Elinor N. Brink, and Dorothea O. Christian, "How to Organize a Friends of the Library" in *Friends of the Library: Organization and Activities*, edited by Sarah Leslie Wallace. Chicago, American Library Association, 1962, pp. 20–29.

first, then the librarian—the latter usually owing his appointment to the former—and later, a Friends group.

Trustees, or the librarian, or the two together may be instrumental in the formation of a Friends group, and may request a local community leader or organization to take the responsibility of calling the initial meeting. Often the librarian takes the initiative. In any case, trustees and the librarian should act with each other's full knowledge, consent, advice, and help.

Citizens themselves, recognizing the need for a Friends group, may take the first steps in starting one. Ideally, the organizers should consult with the librarian and the trustees before launching their venture. By so doing they may gain valuable knowledge as well as assistance in such practical considerations as meeting space and possible staff help. The financial aid—postage, printing, paper, as well as the staff time—that a library can allow the Friends will be controlled by local policies, budgetary restrictions, and in some cases, by legal considerations.

Since all have libraries as their common interest, Friends, trustees, and librarians should have little trouble in working together. To ensure smooth working relations—since all are human—everyone concerned should keep two points in mind. First, appreciation of a job well done must be articulated to be of value. Second, a clear understanding must be maintained of the responsibilities and function of each. Both librarian and trustees have definite duties and powers, often prescribed by law. These cannot be appropriated by the Friends. On the other hand, there are areas in which Friends operate far more effectively than either librarian or trustee. To each his own, then, but with each working under the umbrella of mutual understanding.

Once organized, Friends should keep the trustees and the administration informed of their program. This is sometimes done by official communications or newsletters. It can also be accomplished by inviting a member of the library board, the librarian, or a staff representative appointed by the librarian to attend the meetings of the Friends and of their board of directors. Some libraries have a staff member designated as the official liaison with the Friends. It is his duty to work with the Friends, advise them, clear matters through channels and act as a link of communication between the Friends and the librarian. The latter in turn is the link to the trustees. The library trustees, on the other hand, should have a definite informational program for the Friends. They should invite the Friends to send an official observer to library board meetings. Only by informing the Friends of their goals, hopes, aspirations, and needs can the trustees gain the profit they should expect from a Friends organization.

No project should be undertaken by the Friends which has not been cleared with the librarian and the trustees. Neither will either of the latter pledge the efforts or the funds of the Friends without first gaining their consent. Most undertakings will be common to all three with lines of activity clearly drawn. A new building is a case in point. Here Friends will take as their major concern the education of the public as to the need for a new building, its meaning to the community, and the basic requirement of broad support, both moral and financial. Friends might also take on a gift campaign for the extras a new building needs but which public funds can seldom provide. Gifts are also in the province of the trustees, however, so a joint program could well be worked out. Trustees will be concerned primarily with the legal aspects of the building, its financing, establishment of the program it will be designed to carry out, letting of contracts and related matters. The librarian and his staff will be the ones most concerned with the detailed planning of the structure and its equipment.

Although practice varies, there is a strong case for the Friends being independent of the library board. That is, trustees should not have membership or a vote in the organization. This exclusion should apply to the staff as well. This separation does not preclude advice or guidance from the trustees or from the librarian and his staff, but it does make the Friends a more effective body when pleading for charter amendments, budget increases, salaries, buildings, and the like. They cannot be accused of self-interest if they are truly an independent group of concerned citizens.

Rare though they be there are instances where library trustees have been derelict in their duty. There have also been librarians who failed to measure up to professional standards. Nor is it unknown for opposition between the trustees and the librarian to reach such proportions that the library and its service to the community were damaged. Friends, independent of ties to either board or administration, have been effective in clearing up such situations and restoring public confidence in the library.

One aspect of the Friends has been overlooked. That is their effectiveness as a training ground for good board members. In a well-organized active group, Friends learn much about the internal workings of a library, its services, its needs, and its goals. With such an education they make logical candidates for the library board.

The Place of Friends in the American Library Association

Although there is a tendency to associate Friends with public libraries, groups of Friends are found in many types of libraries. Public libraries have a good share of Friends, including those grouped around county libraries, community branches, and special libraries. State libraries have their Friends. Colleges and universities rejoice often in closely knit groups which take the enrichment of the collection as their goal. School libraries have their Friends.

All groups, no matter what parent body they cluster about, should enlarge their outlook. Like librarians and trustees, Friends can do a better job if they become aware of the national—even the international—library scene. In talking to people from other cities, other states, other regions, they discover that their own problems are not unique, that some of them have been met successfully elsewhere, that others are still unsolved. They find an educated sounding board against which they can try out their ideas.

Most groups of Friends are looking for a means of exchange between themselves and other groups. This exchange, this meeting place of like-minded people, this sounding board is found in the American Library Association. Librarians and trustees, always active in the Association, should urge their Friends group to join, either as an organization or as individuals, for the wider understanding of libraries that membership will give them. And the more numerous Friends become in the Association, the more useful it can become to them as they take part in its activities and planning.

A Friends of Libraries Committee exists in the Public Relations Section of the Library Administration Division of the American Library Association, and many state level organizations of Friends have been formed.

Even so, it is significant and important that local Friends groups are unfettered by state or national supervision or controls. They are free to adapt their activities to the changing needs of their particular libraries in accordance with the desires of the trustees and the librarians. All three are dedicated to the same prime objective: to provide the community with the kind of library and with the best library services suitable to the community requirements.

Chapter Twenty

Trustees Working Together: State, Regional, and National Associations

BY ALICE B. IHRIG

AND EDWARD G. STRABLE

Library trusteeship in its essence is a *group* activity since the basic framework within which each trustee performs his function is the library board. From its inception, then, this type of endeavor has required trustees to develop techniques of cooperation, interaction, coordination, representation, and all the other group relationships which prevail when people work together for a common cause.

At the same time, although the focus of trustee activity has typically and traditionally been the individual community and its library needs and aspirations, the point-of-view has been enlarging in the past

MRS. IHRIG is President of the Board of Trustees of the Oak Lawn (Ill.) Public Library, and has served as acting Executive Secretary, American Library Trustee Association.

MR. STRABLE is Manager, Information Services, J. Walter Thompson Company, Chicago, and has served as Executive Secretary, American Library Trustee Association.

decades, along with the movement toward larger units of library service, to encompass broader horizons. The county, the state, the region, and the nation have become additional points of focus for trustees.

It is not surprising, then, to find trustees in organized groups larger than the local library board and actively engaged in the process of identifying, attacking, and solving library problems which affect larger geographic areas.

The traditional relationship of the lay board and the professional library staff working together as partners in the community to solve common problems has been carried over into association activity, with each handling those functions it can most effectively perform. Structurally, associations of trustees are most often an integral part of the library associations of the state, region, or country. But even in those instances in which the trustee group organizes as a separate entity, the relationships with the organization of librarians are close and strong.

This chapter attempts to give a brief and broad picture of how and why trustees work together beyond the board level.

State Associations

Since trustees are, in most parts of most states, the policy makers for their public libraries, they carry great responsibility for the growth of library services in their communities, and through their communities, the growth of library services in the states. Trustees in 47 states have formed associations to work together.[1]

Whether divisions or sections of state library associations, or independent units, the trustee groups tend to have similar primary purposes. The first—the provision of good library service to every citizen of the state—is an objective they share with the rest of the library profession of the state. The second purpose is most often expressed as "education of the individual library trustee." In pursuit of the first objective the trustee groups play their proper roles in the activities of the state library associations and the state library agencies. In pursuit of the second, the trustee associations plan conferences, workshops, and other types of meetings for their trustee members. Most have regular bulletins or news sheets. Some publish trustee handbooks, develop codes of ethics for trustees and suggested policy statements for library boards, and similar activities.

[1] Barbara B. Holden. *The State Trustee Organization,* Chicago, American Library Trustee Association, 1968.

State trustee associations have had varied success in reaching objectives as well as in the programs of activities which they have developed. The most thorough study of these associations to be made in recent years was undertaken in 1967–68 by the American Library Trustee Association (ALTA), the trustee division of the American Library Association.

ALTA had long recognized that the most effective organizational contact for a trustee, beyond his own board, comes through a state association. Through a J. Morris Jones—World Book Encyclopedia—ALA Goals Award, ALTA established a project for the purpose of studying state trustee groups, identifying the elements of strength which contribute to effective and successful ones, and communicating these findings to all trustee groups so they might be put into practice. The project took the form of in-person, in-depth interviews with the trustee leadership in eight states where strong trustee activity at the state level had been demonstrated.

To summarize, the study found the following to be some of the most important characteristics of a strong state library trustee association:

Has a workable formal structure (constitution and bylaws) which is understood, followed and yet is flexible.

Exhibits a commitment to clearly stated short-range and long-range objectives.

Has an executive board or committee which meets more often than the general membership and on a regular basis.

Provides regular communications to this executive board as well as to all trustees in the state.

Has a sound committee structure suited to the needs and problems of the organization.

Commands in the state a clear recognition of the role of trustees in library development.

Presents programs at the annual conference, and institutes and workshops, which are planned specifically with the needs of trustees in mind.

Has developed cooperative relationships with the state library agency and the state library association.

Has an ongoing program of activities to carry out goals, reflected in communications, legislation, the initiation of projects, and the recruitment of members and of new leadership.

Has adequate financing.

The characteristics listed above indicate to some degree what state trustee associations are and do. But special attention should be given to three important common areas of activity: trustee education, legislation, and Governor's Conferences on libraries.

Trustee education is a continuing responsibility of state trustee groups which is complicated by the constant turnover in trustees. Associations provide basic publications (trustee manuals, newsletters, bulletins) and plan for programs which help the library trustee serve his local library effectively but also see it as a unit in a larger plan for statewide library development. Information on the directions of library service, the problems of manpower, plans for interlibrary cooperation, financing and taxation, policy setting, etc., are subjects which trustee associations consider with their memberships on a regular and repetitive basis.

Legislation at state and national levels is another continuing requirement if libraries are to grow and find their place in the spectrum of public services. Trustee associations initiate ideas for legislation, cooperate in promoting adoption of needed laws, and help to keep trustees and the public informed. One of the great strengths of trustees is this ability to speak of library needs from the lay citizen viewpoint.

Governor's Conferences on Libraries are a device, closely related to the legislative effort, developed to promote citizen interest in libraries and their problems. Briefly, they are meetings held in a state, with a governor as sponsor and host, to present the library development story to citizen leaders from all areas of the state. They provide a format in which library trustees and librarians can talk to citizens and build support for superior library service.

Perhaps the most significant recognition of the contribution which trustees can make to the library effort at the state level is the election of a trustee to the presidency of the association, a situation which has applied in a number of states in recent years.

Regional Associations

In some areas of the United States, trustees are active on a sectional basis through formally organized regional library associations. These regions usually include several states where geographical and social cohesion provide a traditional working relationship, such as the Pacific

Northwest, Southeast, New England, Southwest, the Mid-Atlantic, and the Midwest areas.

In part, these regional groups are a response to current emphasis on regional library development and interstate cooperation. Through them, librarians and trustees fill the need for drawing on new resources, and planning for the day of universal access to all libraries. The annual meetings of these associations normally involve librarians and trustees in programs and discussions which go beyond the confines of one state. Contacts with their counterparts in neighboring states provide opportunities for sharing ideas about many of the same problems and experiences—thus enlarging the participant's concept of the library role sectionally and nationally. The larger membership rolls and combined financial resources available enable regional associations to arrange programs of unusual value to members.

As trustees across the country become more thoroughly involved in larger units of library service and information networks, it is likely they will turn their attention more directly to regional library associations and to trustee activity at that level.

The National Association

The American Library Association (ALA) is the major library association in the United States, and the American Library Trustee Association (ALTA), which is one of the 14 divisions of ALA, is the only national association of trustees. ALA has existed since 1876. A trustee group has been active in ALA since 1890. ALTA received division status in 1961. Membership in ALTA is open to any ALA member who wishes to join. This includes some librarians, institutional members, and Friends of Libraries; but in large part ALTA's membership consists of public library trustees.

The main objective of the ALA, as stated in its constitution, is "to promote library service and librarianship." Each of the 14 divisions of the ALA represents a field of activity and responsibility clearly distinct from that of other divisions. ALTA's place in this structure as well as its objectives are best summarized in its "statement of responsibility" which is as follows:

> The American Library Trustee Association is interested in the development of effective library service for all people in all types of communities and in all types of libraries; it follows that its members

are concerned as policy makers with organizational patterns of service, with the development of competent personnel, the provision of adequate financing, the passage of suitable legislation, and the encouragement of citizen support for libraries. ALTA recognizes that responsibility for professional action in these fields has been assigned to other divisions of ALA; its specific responsibilities as a division, therefore, are:

1. A continuing and comprehensive educational program to enable the library trustees to discharge their grave responsibilities in a manner best fitted to benefit the public and the libraries they represent.
2. Continuous study and review of the activities of library trustees.
3. Conduct of activities and projects within its area of responsibility.
4. Synthesis of the activities of all units within ALA as they relate to trustees.
5. Stimulation of the development of library trustees, and stimulation of participation by trustees in appropriate type-of-library divisions.
6. Representation and interpretation of the activities of library trustees in contacts outside the library profession, particularly with national organizations and governmental agencies.

The specific programs developed by ALTA to carry out its responsibilities within the ALA vary over time. But an overview of the activities at any point in time finds the Association working in the mainstream of the objectives outlined above.

ALTA's continuing educational program for library trustees is most directly reflected in its publications and annual meetings. *The Public Library Trustee* is the official ALTA newsletter which is issued quarterly to members and which provides not only news of trustee activities but short articles on subjects of general concern—trustee responsibilities, trustee relationship to the library building program, public relations and trustees, etc.—usually written by trustees and always written to the trustee point of view. ALTA has had a close relationship to both editions of the book in hand, which is recognized throughout the library profession as the standard handbook for library trustees.

A concerted effort toward the production of needed publications in recent years has resulted in ALTA publications dealing with the techniques of holding workshops, a discussion of the organization and proper operations of state trustee organizations, a revision of the valuable guidelines on how Governor's Conferences on libraries should be organized and run, and a landmark analysis of the literature of trusteeship which tells how the institution of trusteeship stands at the end of the nineteen sixties.

ALTA's annual conference programs, designed to supplement and strengthen programs held for trustees at the regional, state, and local level, usually deal with subjects which cut across the board of trusteeship. First steps in library automation, federal legislative trends, the changing institution of trusteeship, the work of the President's Commission on Libraries, are examples of recent subjects presented by speakers of national stature.

In legislation, ALTA works through its subcommittee to the ALA Legislation Committee and provides a countrywide network of trustee coordinators to inform and act when appropriate. ALTA leaders are called upon to testify to congressional committees when legislation is pending. In intellectual freedom and in the National Library Week effort it also cooperates on associationwide programs.

In everything it does, ALTA relates back to the state trustee groups through written communications with the leaders of those groups, and, most effectively, through its seven regional directors. These are experienced trustees and members of the Board of Directors who are charged with serving as liaison between ALA and ALTA and the trustee groups in their regions. They are available to help plan programs, suggest speakers, share ideas, explore new program techniques, obtain material, assist in evaluation, suggest methods of strengthening state trustee organizations, to name just a few of the functions regularly performed. ALTA's State Association Committee, on which each regional director is a member, considers new and better methods for cooperation and communication between the national and state levels of trusteeship. It also plans and presents a program at each annual conference of special interest to representatives of the state associations, following up the program meeting with regional meetings where ideas can be shared. This committee works closely with ALTA's Governor's Conference Committee which provides direct aid and advice to state groups planning such conferences.

Trustee members of the ALA also play a larger role in the parent association. Increasingly, in recent years, trustees have been named to ALA committees, such as the Committee on Organization, the Legislation Committee, the Intellectual Freedom Committee, and to working units of other divisions, such as the Library Administration Division and the Public Libraries Association, to inject their point of view and experience into these activities. And there are, finally, trustee members on the ALA Council, which is the governing body of the national association. They represent not just the members of ALTA, but the estimated 61,000 public library trustees on library boards in the U.S.

This final bit of information brings to full circle this brief discussion of trustees working together, a circle which begins and ends with the individual library board and the individual trustee. Throughout this discussion there has been, of course, an implicit invitation to the trustee reader to become some part of this organized effort toward better libraries for all.

Chapter Twenty-One

The Trustee
in Tomorrow's World

BY VIRGINIA G. YOUNG

THE LIBRARY trustee may well find that the world of to-day provides sufficient challenges to test his effort and ingenuity, without trying to pierce the veil of the future. Rapid changes in technological equipment, in building design and function, in publication and reproduction of materials, in shifts of population, in amounts and methods of financing and grants, all pose a bewildering multiplicity of choices and decisions upon the lay trustee in the professional library world.

These problems, however, can be solved, as library boards are proving every day. Study and application, plus adaptability and willingness to learn provide the trustee with the means of solving each new problem. Professional assistance is in ample supply from government and state agencies, and through the American Library Association. Even if the difficult is not done immediately (and the impossible, of course, takes a little longer) it *can* be done.

It is not, therefore, the increasingly complex technological problems which provide the trustee's greatest challenge in the world of to-morrow. As the years of this century crowd by, man's achievements in the technological field grow more and more dazzling. But it also becomes more apparent with every passing year that the viability of our civilization is not rooted in even the most sophisticated equipment or materiel, but in mutual understanding between nations, races, creeds, and individuals. If we have a world to live in tomorrow, it must be a world of person-to-person communication and interaction.

It is in helping to build this world that the library trustee finds an immediate challenge, an incomparable opportunity to serve. Libraries exist by and for the human mind, and it is the human mind which bears the responsibility for what they are. No computerized mathematical projection can replace far-reaching effect of vision prompted by concern.

The challenge of tomorrow's world for the library trustee, indeed, is rooted in the area of human concern. Concern that his library shall offer total service, with particular thought for those disadvantaged economically or physically; concern for good and productive working relationships within the library walls; concern that the library and the community shall be mutual sources of service and support—the trustee who is dedicated to proving these concerns will find that the lesser problems of hardware and housekeeping will fall into their proper perspective.

And that proper place is to serve the library, to furnish the everyday tools for the library's operation. No matter how complex the technological problems nor how grueling the challenge they present, their place is still subordinate to the areas of human concern embodied in the library. From chisel to stylus to pen to movable type, man and his libraries have pressed ever forward, discovering, inventing, and using new tools of learning.

The trustee in tomorrow's world will have a constructive role in the library's long story. Knowing that it is man who plans and operates machines (for people build computers, computers do not build people), tomorrow's trustee will regard technological complexity as merely another tool to his hand—another useful object to serve the library and the mind of man.

But even as today, tomorrow's trustee will need a sense of commitment. John W. Gardner, former Secretary of Health, Education and Welfare, has made the following statement which might be spoken directly to today's as well as tomorrow's trustee:

> "We built this complex dynamic society, and we can make it serve our purposes. We designed this technological civilization, and we can

manage it for our own benefit. If we can build organizations, we can make them serve the individual.

"To do this takes a commitment of mind and heart—as it always did. If we make that commitment, this society will more and more come to be what it was always meant to be: a fit place for the human being to grow and flourish."[1]

[1] John W. Gardner. *No Easy Victories*. Harper and Row, New York, 1968.

Trustee
Orientation Program

The first time an orientation is given, it might be used at a full board meeting. It is recommended, after experimenting with several different methods, that the orientation for new trustees be given in the librarian's office with the chairman of the board or another qualified trustee conducting the meeting. Best results were obtained in small groups which made for more personal and informal meetings.

I. Welcome of New Members to Board

A. Greetings
B. Appointment to board

> CHAIRMAN: We all realize that an appointment to the library board is a public trust. The library is a perfect example today of democracy and of the American ideal of equal opportunity for all. A librarian recently wrote that "the library is the last stronghold of democracy, and it is the one institution that still serves the individual." A trustee or a library board member—and they are synonymous—has the rare opportunity and obligation of promoting this American ideal of equal opportunity for all; therefore, a love of humanity and its educational welfare is a necessary attribute of library trustees.
>
> The board of trustees is responsible for the total effectiveness of the library service and for keeping the public, as well as the government officials, informed of the library's progress and of its needs.
>
> We work directly with community groups as well as with individuals; we obtain assistance for our various projects, and we must see that the

Prepared by American Library Trustee Association, Action Development Committee, 1960. Revised 1963, 1968.

program of the library is adequately understood by the public. We really serve as a two-way radio because we get all of the successes and the failures of the library's program and its service, and we transmit this to the librarian. Also, we should transmit the library's program, its plan, its problems, to the public.

C. Why orientation?

CHAIRMAN: Most of us came on this board rather "green." After seeing the struggle that it took to understand the local, district, state, and national set-up, this board decided to try an orientation program to help new trustees learn about their responsibilities more quickly.

So often people ask, "What can I do for the library?" You should realize that each of you has a talent to give to your library. Perhaps the library desperately needs the very thing that you are capable of doing. Maybe your special field is in business management, or in finance, or personnel, or purchasing, or in public relations, or as a public speaker. We all have something to contribute.

II. Brief History of Local Library

At this point trustees should be given information regarding their library, either orally or in printed material.

Suggestions:

The beginning; the value of property, such as book collection, bookmobile, building and site, etc.;
The financial status, with source of income including local, state and/or federal grants;
A copy of budget;
List of personnel and pay scale;
Latest annual report;
Agendas of a few previous meetings;
Brief review of state library laws.

III. Responsibilities and Duties

A. The responsibility assumed by trustee

CHAIRMAN: When we assume the responsibility of a trustee, we say, "I am interested in my library to the extent that I am willing to serve without compensation for the period of my appointment, to attend board meetings regularly, to accept an office or membership on a committee if called upon to do so, and to fill that office creditably and efficiently without expecting special privileges. My good judgment and common sense, as well as any special ability which I may possess, will be at the service of my library. I shall endeavor to be informed on library trends, on problems of my neighboring libraries as well as my own, and to grow as I help my institution to grow."

B. Read aloud the duties and responsibilities of trustees from local or state handbook. (Also see Chapter Two of Young's *The Library Trustee: A Practical Guidebook.*)

Be sure to clarify that trustees are a policy-determining body for the library and are responsible for obtaining sufficient funds to meet library needs. Summarize the primary responsibilities:

1. Make every one in community aware of the library.
2. Secure adequate financial support.
3. Encourage continued growth and development of library staff. The library is the fourth cornerstone of American civilization and culture—the home, church, school and library. It is a patriotic duty to seek for the community the best library that it can possibly afford.

IV. Trustee Organizations

A. Why trustee associations and conferences are important.

CHAIRMAN: To be a good trustee, one must keep informed on all library services, new programs and projects. Membership in national and state trustee associations and attendance at their meetings are an essential means of doing this. (More information is available in Chapter Twenty of Young's *Guidebook*.)

B. *Regional.* Explain your own state map of regions or districts. Discuss when regional meetings are usually held. They bring together trustees and librarians where common problems are discussed, solutions offered and future plans made.

C. *State.* Give purpose of organization. Discuss membership in state association, the dues, the divisions of state association with emphasis on trustee section and its executive board, and finally the meetings, where state and national matters of concern are discussed and future plans determined.

Annual state library association meetings provide a fine opportunity for trustees to obtain a statewide view of library service, in addition to receiving information and stimulation. Many libraries pay trustees' expenses when they attend state or regional meetings.

D. *National.* The American Library Association is the chief spokes-man for the modern library movement in North America. It is an organization of libraries, librarians, trustees, and Friends of the Library.

> The ALA holds an annual conference each summer in various cities of the United States and Canada, and a midwinter planning conference, with special programs for trustees.
>
> Encourage membership in ALA. Many libraries pay the fee for trustees, as no one may serve on a national committee or hold an office unless he is a member of the ALA.
>
> The American Library Trustee Association (ALTA) is a division of ALA.
>
> List the present officers of ALTA and some of the committees:

Action Development Committee   ALTA State Associations Committee
Governor's Conference   National Library Week
    Committee   Subcommittee
Publications Committee   Legislative Liaison Subcommittee
Membership Subcommittee

V. Complete Tour of Library

Introduce trustees to staff when convenient and possible.

VI. Reading List for Trustees (Appendix No. XI in Young's *Guidebook.*)

Library Bill of Rights

Adopted June 18, 1948

Amended February 2, 1961, and June 27, 1967,

by the ALA Council

The Council of the American Library Association reaffirms its belief in the following basic policies which should govern the services of all libraries.

1. As a responsibility of library service, books and other library materials selected should be chosen for values of interest, information and enlightenment of all the people of the community. In no case should library materials be excluded because of the race or nationality or the social, political, or religious views of the authors.

2. Libraries should provide books and other materials presenting all points of view concerning the problems and issues of our times; no library materials should be proscribed or removed from libraries because of partisan or doctrinal disapproval.

3. Censorship should be challenged by libraries in the maintenance of their responsibility to provide public information and enlightenment.

4. Libraries should cooperate with all persons and groups concerned with resisting abridgment of free expression and free access to ideas.

5. The rights of an individual to the use of a library should not be

---

By official action of the Council on February 3, 1951, the Library Bill of Rights shall be interpreted to apply to all materials and media of communication used or collected by libraries.

denied or abridged because of his age, race, religion, national origins or social or political views.

6. As an institution of education for democratic living, the library should welcome the use of its meeting rooms for socially useful and cultural activities and discussion of current public questions. Such meeting places should be available on equal terms to all groups in the community regardless of the beliefs and affiliations of their members, provided that the meetings be open to the public.

Freedom to Read Statement

Adopted June 25, 1953, by the ALA Council

The freedom to read is essential to our democracy. It is under attack. Private groups and public authorities in various parts of the country are working to remove books from sale, to censor textbooks, to label "controversial" books, to distribute lists of "objectionable" books or authors, and to purge libraries. These actions apparently rise from a view that our national tradition of free expression is no longer valid; that censorship and suppression are needed to avoid the subversion of politics and the corruption of morals. We, as citizens devoted to the use of books and as librarians and publishers responsible for disseminating them, wish to assert the public interest in the preservation of the freedom to read.

We are deeply concerned about these attempts at suppression. Most such attempts rest on a denial of the fundamental premise of democracy: that the ordinary citizen, by exercising his critical judgment, will accept the good and reject the bad. The censors, public and private, assume that they should determine what is good and what is bad for their fellow-citizens.

We trust Americans to recognize propaganda, and to reject obscenity. We do not believe they need the help of censors to assist them in this task. We do not believe they are prepared to sacrifice their heritage of a free press in order to be "protected" against what others think may be bad for them. We believe they still favor free enterprise in ideas and expression.

We are aware, of course, that books are not alone in being subjected to efforts at suppression. We are aware that these efforts are related to a larger pattern of pressures being brought against education, the press, films, radio and television. The problem is not only one of actual censorship. The shadow of fear cast by these pressures leads, we suspect, to an even larger voluntary curtailment of expression by those who seek to avoid controversy.

Such pressure toward conformity is perhaps natural to a time of uneasy change and pervading fear. Especially when so many of our apprehensions are directed against an ideology, the expression of a dissident idea becomes a thing feared in itself, and we tend to move against it as against a hostile deed, with suppression.

And yet suppression is never more dangerous than in such a time of social tension. Freedom has given the United States the elasticity to endure strain. Freedom keeps open the path of novel and creative solutions, and enables change to come by choice. Every silencing of a heresy, every enforcement of an orthodoxy, diminishes the toughness and resilience of our society and leaves it the less able to deal with stress.

Now as always in our history, books are among our greatest instruments of freedom. They are almost the only means for making generally available ideas or manners of expression that can initially command only a small audience. They are the natural medium for the new idea and the untried voice from which come the original contributions to social growth. They are essential to the extended discussion which serious thought requires, and to the accumulation of knowledge and ideas into organized collections.

We believe that free communication is essential to the preservation of a free society and a creative culture. We believe that these pressures towards conformity present the danger of limiting the range and variety of inquiry and expression on which our democracy and our culture depend. We believe that every American community must jealously guard the freedom to publish and to circulate, in order to preserve its own freedom to read. We believe that publishers and librarians have a profound responsibility to give validity to that freedom to read by making it possible for the readers to choose freely from a variety of offerings.

The freedom to read is guaranteed by the Constitution. Those with faith in free men will stand firm on these constitutional guarantees of essential rights and will exercise the responsibilities that accompany these rights.

We therefore affirm these propositions:

1. It is in the public interest for publishers and librarians to make available the widest diversity of views and expressions, including those which are unorthodox or unpopular with the majority.

Creative thought is by definition new, and what is new is different. The bearer of every new thought is a rebel until his idea is refined and tested. Totalitarian systems attempt to maintain themselves in power by the ruthless suppression of any concept which challenges the established orthodoxy. The power of a democratic system to adapt to change is vastly strengthened by the freedom of its citizens to choose widely from among conflicting opinions offered freely to them. To stifle every nonconformist idea at birth would mark the end of the democratic process. Furthermore, only through the constant activity of weighing and selecting can the democratic mind attain the strength demanded by times like these. We need to know not only what we believe but why we believe it.

2. Publishers and librarians do not need to endorse every idea or presentation contained in the books they make available. It would conflict with the public interest for them to establish their own political, moral or aesthetic views as the sole standard for determining what books should be published or circulated.

Publishers and librarians serve the educational process by helping to make available knowledge and ideas required for the growth of the mind and the increase of learning. They do not foster education by imposing as mentors the patterns of their own thought. The people should have the freedom to read and consider a broader range of ideas than those that may be held by any single librarian or publisher or government or church. It is wrong that what one man can read should be confined to what another thinks proper.

3. It is contrary to the public interest for publishers or librarians to determine the acceptability of a book solely on the basis of the personal history or political affiliations of the author.

A book should be judged as a book. No art or literature can flourish if it is to be measured by the political views or private lives of its creators. No society of free men can flourish which draws up lists of writers to whom it will not listen, whatever they may have to say.

4. The present laws dealing with obscenity should be vigorously enforced. Beyond that, there is no place in our society for extralegal ef-

*forts to coerce the taste of others, to confine adults to the reading
matter deemed suitable for adolescents, or to inhibit the efforts of
writers to achieve artistic expression.*

To some, much of modern literature is shocking. But is not much
of life itself shocking? We cut off literature at the source if we prevent
serious artists from dealing with the stuff of life. Parents and teachers
have a responsibility to prepare the young to meet the diversity of
experiences in life to which they will be exposed, as they have a responsibility to help them learn to think critically for themselves. These
are affirmative responsibilities, not to be discharged simply by prevent-
ing them from reading works for which they are not yet prepared. In
these matters taste differs, and taste cannot be legislated; nor can machinery be devised which will suit the demands of one group without
limiting the freedom of others. We deplore the catering to the imma-
ture, the retarded or the maladjusted taste. But those concerned with
freedom have the responsibility of seeing to it that each individual
book or publication, whatever its contents, price or method of distribution, is dealt with in accordance with due process of law.

*5. It is not in the public interest to force a reader to accept with
any book the prejudgment of a label characterizing the book or author
as subversive or dangerous.*

The ideal of labeling presupposes the existence of individuals or
groups with wisdom to determine by authority what is good or bad
for the citizen. It presupposes that each individual must be directed
in making up his mind about the ideas he examines. But Americans do
not need others to do their thinking for them.

*6. It is the responsibility of publishers and librarians, as guardians
of the people's freedom to read, to contest encroachments upon that
freedom by individuals or groups seeking to impose their own standards or tastes upon the community at large.*

It is inevitable in the give and take of the democratic process that
the political, the moral, or the aesthetic concepts of an individual or
group will occasionally collide with those of another individual or
group. In a free society each individual is free to determine for himself what he wishes to read, and each group is free to determine what
it will recommend to its freely associated members. But no group has
the right to take the law into its own hands, and to impose its own

concept of politics or morality upon other members of a democratic society. Freedom is no freedom if it is accorded only to the accepted and the inoffensive.

7. It is the responsibility of publishers and librarians to give full meaning to the freedom to read by providing books that enrich the quality of thought and expression. By the exercise of this affirmative responsibility, bookmen can demonstrate that the answer to a bad book is a good one, the answer to a bad idea is a good one.

The freedom to read is of little consequence when expended on the trivial; it is frustrated when the reader cannot obtain matter fit for his purpose. What is needed is not only the absence of restraint, but the positive provision of opportunity for the people to read the best that has been thought and said. Books are the major channel by which the intellectual inheritance is handed down, and the principal means of its testing and growth. The defense of their freedom and integrity, and the enlargement of their service to society, requires of all bookmen the utmost of their faculties, and deserves of all citizens the fullest of their support.

We state these propositions neither lightly nor as easy generalizations. We here stake out a lofty claim for the value of books. We do so because we believe that they are good, possessed of enormous variety and usefulness, worthy of cherishing and keeping free. We realize that the application of these propositions may mean the dissemination of ideas and manners of expression that are repugnant to many persons. We do not state these propositions in the comfortable belief that what people read is unimportant. We believe rather that what people read is deeply important; that ideas can be dangerous; but that the suppression of ideas is fatal to a democratic society. Freedom itself is a dangerous way of life, but it is ours.

Endorsed by:
AMERICAN LIBRARY ASSOCIATION

Council, June 25, 1953

AMERICAN BOOK PUBLISHERS COUNCIL
Board of Directors, June 18, 1953

Subsequently Endorsed by:
AMERICAN BOOKSELLERS ASSOCIATION
Board of Directors

BOOK MANUFACTURERS' INSTITUTE
Board of Directors
NATIONAL EDUCATION ASSOCIATION
Commission for the
Defense of Democracy through Education

Appendix IV

Guidelines for a Library Policy

BY ELIZABETH A. KINGSEED

General Library Objectives

General library objectives to be considered should include:

1. Promote enlightened citizenship
2. Enrich personal lives
3. Encourage continuous self-education
4. Seek to identify community needs
5. Assume a leadership role in the community
6. Support Library Bill of Rights and Freedom to Read Statement
7. Assemble, preserve, and administer books and related materials
8. Serve the community as a center of reliable information
9. Provide free service to every resident in community

Services of the Library

The library provides books and materials for information, entertainment, intellectual development, and enrichment of the people of the community. The library should endeavor to:

1. Select, organize, and make available necessary books and materials
2. Provide guidance and assistance to borrowers
3. Initiate programs, exhibits, book lists, etc.
4. Cooperate with other community agencies and organizations
5. Secure information beyond its own resources when requested

MISS KINGSEED is Assistant State Librarian, New Hampshire State Library.

6. Lend to other libraries upon request
7. Provide special services to nonresidents, disadvantaged, blind, hospital patients, etc.
8. Maintain a balance in its services to various age groups
9. Cooperate with, but not perform the functions of, school or other institutional libraries
10. Provide service during hours which best meet the needs of the community
11. Provide service outlets located at points of maximum interest
12. Periodically review library service being offered

Budget

The following points should be considered in a policy on budgets:

1. Preparation—who is responsible
2. Scope—items to be included and percentages to be used for different categories
3. Presentation—by whom and when
4. Special budget for new construction or capital improvements is needed

Personnel

The main points of good personnel policy include the following:

1. A description of each job in the library, degree of responsibility, educational and other qualifications required, special abilities or skills required, and the salary scale attached to the job
2. A regular salary scale, giving minimum and maximum salary or wages, amount of increments, period between increments, etc.
3. Provision for provisional appointment with specified length of probation
4. Comfortable working conditions—adequate heat, light, rest rooms, etc.
5. Vacation with pay
6. Sick leave with pay
7. A regular work week with specified number of hours
8. Regular holidays granted other public employees in community
9. Work breaks

10. Social security and fringe benefits available to other public employees—hospitalization, other insurance, pension plans, and workmen's compensation coverage
11. Tenure—protection against unfair discharge or demotion
12. Attendance at library meetings—time off with pay and travel expenses
13. Opportunities for further training with pay, if possible
14. Resignation—amount of notice required and stipulation that resignation should be in writing
15. Provision for hiring substitute librarian when needed
16. Statement on responsibility of librarian for administration of library and responsibility of trustees for making library policy

It is recommended that the policy carry the approval of the local government body to avoid misunderstandings over such matters as salaries and tenure.

Book Selection

1. Support of Library Bill of Rights and Freedom to Read Statement
2. Who is responsible for selection
3. Quality of books to be selected
4. Scope, emphasis, and limits of collection
5. Treatment of gifts
6. Basis for withdrawals and disposal of discards
7. Position on supplying textbooks, primers, and other materials related to school curriculum

The best selection statement should reflect the philosophy and overall objectives of the library.

Cooperation with Other Libraries

A policy on cooperation should include statements on:

1. Recognition of need for cooperation
2. Affiliation with Statewide Library Development Plan
3. Kinds of libraries with which library should cooperate
4. Areas of cooperation

Public Relations

Some of the primary public relations goals of the library should be:

1. To inform the public of library objectives and services through the press, radio, TV, etc.
2. Recognition of part played by staff, trustees, and Friends of the Library in public relations
3. Participation by staff in community activities
4. Responsibility of staff for making talks in the community
5. To encourage use of the library
6. To obtain citizen support for library development

Gifts and Special Collections

Gifts can help promote the program of the library, but libraries have found it helpful to point to an established policy, especially when books and other articles are offered. A policy should include statements on:

1. Conditions under which gifts of books and other materials will be accepted
2. Disposition of non-usable gifts
3. Acceptance of personal property, art objects, portraits, etc.
4. Conditions under which gifts of money, real property and/or stock will be accepted
5. Shelving of special collections
6. Use of special bookplates
7. Acceptance of denominational literature
8. Acceptance of historical materials and writings of local authors
9. Storage of material not designated as an outright gift
10. Encouragement of gifts for memorial purposes

Relationships with Schools

The public library and the public school are companion educational agencies, but their responsibilities differ in scope and function. In writing a policy the library should:

1. Define the separate functions and objectives of the public library and the school library
2. Determine ways of establishing cooperative relations with the school
3. Provide for continuous joint planning between those responsible for school and public library service
4. Provide a written contract if library is to give full service to schools

Use of Library by Groups

Libraries have found it useful to adopt a written policy stating:

1. Who may use the rooms and when
2. Whether a fee will be charged, and if so, how much
3. Whether janitor service will be provided
4. Whether meetings are to be free to the public
5. Whether smoking will be allowed
6. What restrictions are needed for regularly scheduled meetings
7. Whether refreshments may be served
8. Whether library activities have priority
9. Who is in charge of reservations

The check list above suggests items which should be included in every library's policy statement but adapted to suit local conditions and needs. Policy must express a true commitment of service and leadership.

Book Selection Policy

The following is one example of a book selection policy:

The board of this library recognizing the pluralistic nature of this community and the varied backgrounds and needs of all citizens, regardless of race, creed or political persuasion, declares as a matter of book selection policy that:

1. Books and/or library material selection is and shall be vested in the librarian and under his direction such members of the professional staff who are qualified by reason of education and training. Any book and/or library material so selected shall be held to be selected by the board.

2. Selection of books and/or other library material shall be made on the basis of their value of interest, information and enlightenment of all people of the community. No book and/or library material shall be excluded because of the race, nationality or the political or social views of the author.

3. This board believes that censorship is a purely individual matter and declares that while anyone is free to reject for himself books which he does not approve of, he cannot exercise this right of censorship to restrict the freedom to read of others.

4. This board defends the principles of the freedom to read and declares that whenever censorship is involved no book and/or library material shall be removed from the library save under the orders of a court of competent jurisdiction.

5. This board adopts and declares that it will adhere to and support:
    a. The Library Bill on Rights, and
    b. The Freedom to Read Statement adopted by the American Library Association,
both of which are made a part hereof.

Budget Check List

The Library Budget Buys Service

A. Salaries

	Current Year	Next Year
Professional	_____	_____
Clerical	_____	_____
Janitorial	_____	_____
Total	_____	_____

1. Has the salary schedule been reviewed recently for increased cost of living adjustments?
2. Have provisions been made for added positions on the staff?
3. Have the annual increments been added to this year's salaries in order to get next year's salaries?
4. Has provision been made for pensions and social security?

B. Books and Other Library Materials

	Current Year	Next Year
Books	_____	_____
Periodicals	_____	_____
Binding	_____	_____
Pamphlets, etc.	_____	_____
Recordings	_____	_____
Films, Film Strips	_____	_____
Other	_____	_____
Total	_____	_____

Prepared by: Public and School Library Services Bureau
Division of the State Library, Archives and History
New Jersey State Department of Education

1. Does the library written book selection policy include proportions of the book budget to be spent for adult, juvenile, fiction, non-fiction, reference?
2. Does the periodical budget include subscriptions to professional journals and book selection tools?

C. Supplies

	Current Year	Next Year
Library Supplies		
Janitorial Supplies		
Other		
Total		

1. Are printed catalog cards included with library supplies?

D. Maintenance

	Current Year	Next Year
Heat		
Light		
Telephone		
Insurance		
Rent		
Other		
Total		

1. Does the insurance cover the books, the catalog, the furniture, and the equipment as well as the building?

E. Equipment

	Current Year	Next Year

1. What equipment, such as typewriters or mimeograph, should be replaced?
2. Should mechanical charging be considered?
3. What new equipment would help provide better service?

F. Public Relations

	Current Year	Next Year
Printed Materials	_____	_____
Posters	_____	_____
Children's Book Week	_____	_____
National Library Week Supplies	_____	_____
Other	_____	_____
Total	_____	_____

1. Will more funds be needed next year than were used this year?

G. Travel

	Current Year	Next Year
Staff Attendance at Professional Meetings	_____	_____
Trustee Attendance at Professional Meetings	_____	_____
Other	_____	_____
Total	_____	_____

H. Capital Improvements

Current Year	Next Year
_____	_____

I. Miscellaneous

Current Year	Next Year
_____	_____

1. Were there any emergencies this year?

TOTAL LIBRARY BUDGET

Current Year	Next Year
_____	_____

SOURCES OF INCOME

	Current Year	Next Year
Tax Support	_____	_____
State Library Aid	_____	_____
Gifts or Bequests	_____	_____
Other	_____	_____
Total	_____	_____

1. Were the bequests given for a specific use?
2. Should the state aid be used for a special project, or should it be used to increase the funds available in any of the above categories?

Sample Bylaws

Article I—Name

This organization shall be called "The Board of Trustees of the ＿＿＿＿＿ Library" existing by virtue of the provisions of Chapter ＿＿＿＿＿ of the Laws of the State of ＿＿＿＿＿, and exercising the powers and authority and assuming the responsibilities delegated to it under the said statute.

Article II—Officers

Section 1. The officers shall be a president, a vice president, a secretary, and a treasurer, elected from among the appointed trustees at the annual meeting of the board.

Section 2. A nominating committee shall be appointed by the president three months prior to the annual meeting who will present a slate of officers at the annual meeting. Additional nominations may be made from the floor.

Section 3. Officers shall serve a term of one year from the annual meeting at which they are elected and until their successors are duly elected.

Section 4. The president shall preside at all meetings of the board, authorize calls for any special meetings, appoint all committees, execute all documents authorized by the board, serve as an ex-officio voting member of all committees, and generally perform all duties associated with that office.

Section 5. The vice president, in the event of the absence or disability of the president, or of a vacancy in that office, shall assume and perform the duties and functions of the president.

Section 6. The secretary shall keep a true and accurate record of all meetings of the board, shall issue notice of all regular and special meetings, and shall perform such other duties as are generally associated with that office.

Section 7. The treasurer shall be the disbursing officer of the board, co-sign all checks, and shall perform such duties as generally devolve upon the office. He shall be bonded in an amount as may be required by a resolution of the board. In the absence or inability of the treasurer, his duties shall be performed by such other members of the board as the board may designate.

Article III—Meetings

Section 1. The regular meetings shall be held each month, the date and hour to be set by the board at its annual meeting.

Section 2. The annual meeting, which shall be for the purpose of the election of officers and the adoption of an annual report, shall be held at the time of the regular meeting in ____(month)____ of each year.

Section 3. The order of business for regular meetings shall include, but not be limited to, the following items which shall be covered in the sequence shown so far as circumstances will permit:

    (a) Roll call of members
    (b) Disposition of minutes of previous regular meeting and any intervening special meeting
    (c) Director's financial report of the library
    (d) Action on bills
    (e) Progress and service report of director
    (f) Committee reports
    (g) Communications
    (h) Unfinished business
    (i) New business

(j) Public presentation to, or discussion with, the board

(k) Adjournment

Section 4. Special meetings may be called by the secretary at the direction of the president, or at the request of ＿＿＿ members, for the transaction of business as stated in the call for the meeting.

Section 5. A quorum for the transaction of business at any meeting shall consist of ＿＿＿ members of the board present in person.

Section 6. Conduct of meetings: Proceedings of all meetings shall be governed by *Robert's Rules of Order*.

Article IV—Library Director and Staff

The board shall appoint a qualified library director who shall be the executive and administrative officer of the library on behalf of the board and under its review and direction. The director shall recommend to the board the appointment and specify the duties of other employees and shall be held responsible for the proper direction and supervision of the staff, for the care and maintenance of library property, for an adequate and proper selection of books in keeping with the stated policy of the board, for the efficiency of library service to the public and for its financial operation within the limitations of the budgeted appropriation. In the case of part-time or temporary employees, the director shall have interim authority to appoint without prior approval of the board provided that any such appointment shall be reported to the board at its next regular meeting.

Article V—Committees

Section 1. The president shall appoint committees of one or more members each for such specific purposes as the business of the board may require from time to time. The committee shall be considered to be discharged upon the completion of the purpose for which it was appointed and after the final report is made to the board.

Section 2.   All committees shall make a progress report to the library board at each of its meetings.

Section 3.   No committee will have other than advisory powers unless, by suitable action of the board, it is granted specific power to act.

Article VI—General

Section 1.   An affirmative vote of the majority of all members of the board present at the time shall be necessary to approve any action before the board. The president may vote upon and may move or second a proposal before the board.

Section 2.   The bylaws may be amended by the majority vote of all members of the board provided written notice of the proposed amendment shall have been mailed to all members at least ten days prior to the meeting at which such action is proposed to be taken.

Section 3.   Any rule or resolution of the board, whether contained in these bylaws or otherwise, may be suspended temporarily in connection with business at hand, but such suspension, to be valid, may be taken only at a meeting at which two-thirds (_____) of the members of the board shall be present and two-thirds of those present shall so approve.

Appendix VII

Library Service to the Disadvantaged: An Outline of Aids for Trustees

BY DOROTHY S. McALLISTER

A. Questions the library board should consider in reviewing goals and policies:

Goals

    1. Do they give, as the overall goal, adequate library service for *all* people in the community, i.e., for such groups as the culturally disadvantaged, the underprivileged, the aging, and the handicapped?

    2. Do they make basic adult education a major goal, especially literacy training?

    3. Do they emphasize the importance of reaching out to previously unserved people?

Policies

    1. Do they seek to fulfill the library needs of the total community, i.e., do they provide for:

        a. *Materials* suited to the use of the economically and culturally deprived, including members of minority and other special groups, as well as of the traditional library user;

        b. *Programs* to attract the unmotivated, and to aid the poor and the undereducated, as well as the out-of-work and out-of-school adult;

    c. *Facilities* that are accessible and inviting, such as neighborhood library or reading centers (either special library extension services financed by LSCA funds or library participation in neighborhood centers in cooperation with other agencies, or as part of a community action program, financed by OEO funds); mobile vans or bookmobiles in large metropolitan and rural areas (in some states, they are needed to reach migrant agricultural workers).

2. In meeting the need for additional personnel to fill new demands, do the policies provide for:

    a. An opportunity for employment and advancement of the disadvantaged (including minorities) and in-service training?

    b. The use of volunteer assistance (for example, as story tellers or as library guides)?

    c. Assignment of workers to the library by the Economic Opportunity Agencies (such as Work-Study and Work-Training Programs, Job Corps, etc.)?

B. Information the trustee should secure:

1. In his community, the number of illiterates[1]; of Negroes, Spanish-Americans, American Indians, and members of other minority groups; of migrants from rural and other areas; of those below the poverty line[2] (an income of $3,300 or less for a family of four);

2. The anti-poverty programs offered or planned by the Community Action Committee and local government agencies;

3. Ways in which the library can supplement the programs of private and public agencies for the disadvantaged, including unemployed youths and school drop-outs;

4. Successful projects and programs conducted by other libraries for special groups[3];

5. Financial aid available for libraries from the federal government, especially the provisions of the

       Economic Opportunity Act

       Library Services and Construction Act

---

[1] Data available from U.S. Census Bureau or local school administrators.

[2] Data available from local welfare or municipal agencies.

[3] See pamphlet, "Neighborhood Library Centers and Services," National Book Committee, One Park Avenue, New York, N.Y. 10016. See also *ALA Bulletin*, *Library Journal*, and various ALA Division bulletins.

Elementary and Secondary Education Act

Higher Education Act

Manpower Training and Development Act

C. Ways trustees can ascertain the library needs of the total community:

1. Talk with people representing different groups in the population: professional, business, labor, educational, minority, the disadvantaged, the rebellious youth, and to people representing all sections of the city, including the poorest.
   a. Do they use the library? If not, why not?
   b. What improvements and new services would they suggest?
2. Meet with the leaders or groups representing the disadvantaged to learn:
   a. What are the barriers to library use by minorities and by the poor?
   b. What services and programs would they themselves like to have? (Note: The Rochester, New York, Library System conducted a special project to investigate the needs of, and literature for, the disadvantaged and to try a variety of approaches and projects.)
   c. What materials (books, films, records, art, etc.) would they themselves find useful?

D. Steps to effective library service to the disadvantaged:

1. Library participation in the overall community planning; (In Detroit, library branches were included among the facilities proposed in the application for a Model Cities Grant. However, with a few exceptions, libraries have not been a part of the overall community planning.)
2. Coordination of the library's programs with those of private and government agencies (federal, state, and local) in the community educational and anti-poverty efforts, with a view to supplementing their work;
3. Cooperation of the library with community action and other agencies, thus extending its usefulness to those agencies and making possible a joint sponsorship of special programs and projects (for instance, sponsorship with the schools of a program to teach illiterates or with community action agencies in making available materials in such projects as Head Start).

E. Methods by which library boards can inform themselves and others regarding services and programs needed by all groups in the community:

    1. A discussion sponsored by the library board, open to the public, with representatives of public and private anti-poverty, welfare, educational, and municipal agencies participating;

    2. A workshop for trustees of the area on promoting and encouraging library use by the culturally deprived and underprivileged.

F. Articles, studies, and reports important to trustees in determining policies and initiating services to the disadvantaged:

General

Report of the ALA Special Committee on "Freedom of Access to Libraries," 1968, a guide for planning action and/or study programs for the widest use of libraries by all segments of society. *ALA Bulletin,* July–August, 1968, pp. 883–86. Single copies 50¢. Write ALA Publishing Dept., 50 E. Huron St., Chicago, Ill. 60611.

"Neighborhood Library Centers and Services," a study by the National Book Committee for the Office of Economic Opportunity, 1967, published by The National Book Committee, Inc., One Park Avenue, New York, New York 10016. Limited quantities free on request at this address. Includes selected studies of library-related programs; analysis of staffing, programming, materials, locations; conclusions as to effective patterns of special services.

Federal Legislation

"Federal Library Legislation, Programs and Services, II," a series of articles by staff members of the U.S. Office of Education, *ALA Bulletin,* October 1967. Single copies of this special section available free from the Office of the Deputy Executive Director, ALA, 50 E. Huron St., Chicago, Ill. 60611. 25 copies, $3.75; 50 copies, $7.50; 100 copies, $15.00

"Libraries and the War on Poverty: Relevant Federal Legislative Programs," *ALA Bulletin,* January 1965. Reprints available from

Adult Services Division, ALA, 50 East Huron Street, Chicago, Illinois 60611.

Illiteracy

"Library Trustees and the Literate Society," by Craig T. Senft (Trustee of the Ridgewood, New Jersey, Library), *ALA Bulletin*, October 1966. Steps in planning illiteracy programs. Single reprints free from ALTA, 50 East Huron Street, Chicago, Illinois 60611.

"Public Library Service for the Functionally Illiterate: A Survey of Practice," edited by Peter Hiatt and Henry Drennan, Public Library Association, ALA. Price, $1.00. This includes an outline of a one-day workshop.

"Service to Adult Illiterates: Guidelines for Librarians," a brochure prepared by Adult Services Division, ASD Committee on Reading Improvement for Adults, ALA. Participation in the community adult education effort. Single copies free from ASD, 50 E. Huron St., Chicago, Illinois 60611.

Library Projects and Programs
for the Disadvantaged

"Neighborhood Library Centers and Services," by the National Book Committee, Inc. Includes description of 10 successful projects by public libraries or library systems, or in cooperation with community agencies. Available free in limited quantities from The National Book Committee, Inc., One Park Avenue, New York, New York 10016.

"Inventory of Library Programs for Disadvantaged Youth," Young Adult Services Division, ALA. Included as one of the "working papers" for the institute "Two Blocks Apart" held at Sarah Lawrence College, July 8–10, 1966. The set of "working papers" available from YASD, 50 E. Huron St., Chicago, Illinois, 60611, at $2.00.

"Operation Head Start," the Queens Borough, New York Public Library Program for Bookless Homes, 1966. Available from the

Library at 89–11 Merrick Boulevard, Jamaica, Queens, New York, 11432.

"Making the Summer Count: A Librarian's Guide to Activities for Young People," prepared by staff of ALA in cooperation with the President's Council on Youth Opportunity. Available free from ALA Office of the Deputy Executive Director, 50 E. Huron Street, Chicago, Illinois, 60611.

"News Notes: Library Service to the Disadvantaged Child," May 1968. Types of service to disadvantaged children in libraries across the country. Children's Services Division, ALA. Free. 50 E. Huron Street, Chicago, Illinois, 60611.

Statement of Brooklyn Public Library Board of Trustees

The Board of Trustees of the Brooklyn Public Library recognizes the rapid and complex pattern of social, economic, cultural and technological change continuing to take place in Brooklyn. These changes have direct implication for library services. They will continue to shape both the demands made on the library and the nature of the library's response. Specifically affecting the role of the public library, both quantitatively and qualitatively, are the following phenomena:

— The continued in-migration of the culturally and economically disadvantaged, most of whom are not oriented to the effective use of books and the rewards of reading.

— The continued out-migration of the well-educated middle class who are active consumers of information and who comprise the majority of those who buy, borrow and use books and other media of communication.

— The increasing number of advanced students and technical specialists whose needs for immediate access to reliable information are more complex and more expensive to meet than are those of the more traditional users of the public library.

— The increasing need for expanded formal education and for more continuous training and retraining of individuals which will result in almost universal participation in some aspect of the educational process.

— The proliferation of activities which generate huge increases in recorded knowledge and communication will require new techniques for organizing and providing access to information.

— The rapid improvement of school and academic libraries which can meet more appropriately than the public library the curriculum-based needs of students and which will permit more effective inter-library cooperation among libraries of different types.

— Advances in electronic data processing which will allow the storage, handling and retrieval of information in a variety of new forms.

— Advances in communications technology which will permit information transfer faster and more efficiently than do existing techniques. These changes will build upon present advances in paperback publishing, the growth in book club merchandising and the ability of the affluent to acquire materials, in various media, for individual use.

An analysis of these and other relevant trends suggests that the public library must redesign its activities and programs if it is to function effectively in the years ahead. Special note, however, should be given to the fact that these trends do not invalidate the basic objectives of the public library. What they do suggest is a re-ordering of emphasis so that the need of each individual for information on which to make his own decisions is fully recognized. Special priority is required for those efforts by the library to reach out to those who cannot or do not take full advantage of the public library. The major long-range goals of the Brooklyn Public Library may be summarized as follows: to select, acquire, organize and promote the use of a broad range of communications media. These materials are provided:

— To meet the individual's need for information whatever the role he is fulfilling in the community.

— To help the individual attain maximum self-development through life-long intellectual and cultural growth, including the use of the library to advance comprehension, promote communication and improve the skills of reading, viewing and listening.

— To supplement the educational experience of individuals whether they are undertaking formal courses of study or are engaged in informal self-education.

— To provide the means for thoughtful and productive participation by groups and individuals in the affairs of the community, the nation and the world.

— To support educational, governmental, cultural and economic activities within the community.

— To encourage productive diversity and to accommodate the library needs of a changing, dynamic heterogeneous urban community.

— To offer to all a diverse recreational experience for the wholesome use of leisure time.

In the light of the trends and changes mentioned above, the Board of Trustees endorses the following types of activities as being consistent with the goals and policies of the Brooklyn Public Library:

I. Promote maximum access to library facilities and resources through:

A. Simplifying and streamlining the processes of borrower registration and circulation control.

B. Increasing the efficiency of acquisition and cataloging so that new materials are available to users as promptly as possible.

C. Improved site selection so that agencies are more highly visible and occupy locations at high volume pedestrian traffic points.

D. Improved construction design to eliminate physical barriers to the handicapped or infirm and to present to all an attractive and inviting exterior.

E. Increasing the hours of service in each agency for maximum convenience to users. Pilot projects for such extended service schedules are endorsed as a means toward securing the required additional funds.

F. Refining and extending the District Library plan so that reading centers can better serve as active distribution points at widespread, highly accessible locations. The District Library itself should continue to serve as the resource for meeting a high proportion of the needs of the highly motivated, more specialized user.

II. Promote maximum awareness and use of the library by all Brooklyn residents through:

A. Expanded public information programs, conducted throughout the Borough, to develop a widespread awareness of the services of the library and their value to the individual.

B. Expanding the efforts of the library to reach out to those individuals and groups who can profit by use of the library.

III. Develop more effective, more flexible, administrative techniques which may better respond to changing conditions by:

A. Conducting studies of library use and experimenting with physical layouts and interior decoration of branches, more appropriate location and shelving arrangement of all types of materials, and devising new library programs for individuals and groups.

B. Offering greater administrative latitude for initiative and innovation at the District Library level so that activities and procedures can reflect the special characteristics of particular neighborhoods.

C. Revising policies affecting the selection and availability of materials so that changing demands are promptly recognized and reflected in the collection.

D. Achieving closer liaison with publishers and other producers of materials to assist in the development of new library materials and equipment, giving particular attention to those persons who do not read well or who are learning English as a second language.

E. Exploring more effective cooperation among libraries of all types through active participation in joint library ventures at the local, state, regional and national levels. New emphasis should be given to co-ordinated working relationships with school and college libraries in Brooklyn and with the New York and Queens Borough Public Libraries.

F. Devising more accurate and more relevant measures of both the quality and quantity of library use so that meaningful cost analysis can be undertaken.

G. Participating with institutions of formal instruction in programs designed to help adults learn to read.

H. Develop more systematic, more efficient in-service training programs for both professional and clerical staff so that users may quickly and easily obtain materials appropriate to their interests and ability.

Forming a Friends Group

Why Organize?

A need for Friends may arise in the community which has an inadequate building or book collection, limited services, insufficient or poorly paid staff, or insufficient funds for acquisition and upkeep. Where library size keeps pace with public demand, it may be that all citizens are not utilizing library facilities to the utmost, and a program to promote and extend library use is desirable.

Who Takes the Initiative?

An organized lay group, such as the Association of University Women or a local service club, can inaugurate a Friends through expansion of its existing committee on civic improvement or community affairs. Or the mayor, the librarian, or library trustees may invite public-spirited citizens to form a study group and initiate a Friends movement. An individual may provide the original impetus for any of these methods, or may simply call together, for a pre-organizational meeting, like-minded citizens who require no sponsoring agent. The strongest Friends, however, are those who anticipate close cooperation with other community groups including local government and with the professional library staff.

Prepared by: Friends of California Libraries, Inc.

What Is the Pre-Organizational Meeting?

"When it is desired to form a permanent society, those interested in it should consult together before calling a meeting to organize the society."[1] This suggests an aura of smoke-filled rooms or coffee-klatch, but is eminently practical.

Essentially, a small group of people resolve, informally, "That a Friends of the Library of this City be formed to (accomplish certain stated aims)." This will be the statement you present to the public through newspapers and individual announcements that a Friends of the Library is forming.

Having stated, to yourselves, your reasons for forming, determine who should be invited to attend the organizational meeting, and where and when it should be held. Select a secretary pro-tem and a chairman pro-tem.

You may now appoint: (1) a bylaws committee which will prepare bylaws for approval at the organizational meeting[2] and (2) a nominating committee, instructed to draw up a slate of officers for presentation at the organizational meeting. You may also want to determine what other committees should be established. Instruct the secretary pro-tem to send out notices stating time and place of the organizational meeting.

Organizational Meeting: Who Comes and What Takes Place?

Invite the public at large, through newspaper stories and a poster or handbills in the library, schools, and community center. Write, quoting your resolution to every organized group on the local chamber of commerce list, urging them to send one official representative and as many other members as can come. Include every club, league, guild, post, and parish. The library is the one public institution designed to be used by everyone, all his life long. Your membership must be open to all, and a Friends group which is inadvertently exclusive is weaker because of it.

At your organizational meeting, outline the purposes and the plans

[1] *Robert's Rules of Order Revised,* pp. 284–291, details the steps to be taken in establishing an organization.
[2] See FCL Sample Bylaws and *Taxation & Incorporation.*

of the Friends group. If you have no FCL Extension Committee speaker to do this, your chairman pro-tem should speak, quoting statistics and established facts to show definite community need for a Friends group.

Follow immediately with the next procedural step: "Mr. Chairman?" "The chair recognizes Mrs. X." "I wish to make the following resolution: 'That it is the sense of this meeting that a Friends of the Library be formed to . . . etc.'" Discussion should follow, and the resolution, possibly amended, be put to the vote and passed.

If your bylaws committee was appointed, the meeting then moves on to hear, debate, and adopt the bylaws. That done, procedure as specified in the bylaws must be followed, and the nominating committee may now be called on to place the slate of officers in nomination.

All those present who signed as members and are therefore qualified to vote, may then elect the officers and board. The chairman pro-tem and secretary pro-tem will turn over gavel and pen, respectively, and the meeting can continue with the appointment of committeemen.

Just prior to entertaining the motion to adjourn to another date and place, the president can assert that he will expect proposals of action from each committee at the next meeting, and then Friends will be truly underway.

If you adhere to more formal procedure, you may do nothing more at your pre-organizational meeting than state reasons for forming; appoint a secretary and chairman pro-tem; and plan the organizational meeting.

Then, at your organizational meeting, you will (1) present the resolution that "a Friends . . . be formed to . . . ," discuss it and vote on it; (2) nominate and elect or appoint a chairman and committee to draft bylaws; (3) appoint a nominating committee; and (4) move that this meeting be adjourned to a future time and place at which officers will be elected, bylaws adopted, committees appointed, and minutes of the organizational meeting be read. The chair may request that all who are present sign up as charter members of the new Friends of the Library, and then entertain a motion for adjournment. You are launched.

Appendix X

The Library's Long Story

BY GEORGE W. GRILL

The Trustee's Place in History

A library trustee is an individual who has been chosen to participate in the administration of one of the oldest and most significant civilizing influences in the history of the human race. There is but little doubt that back of all libraries, both ancient and modern, there have been trustees, governors, committees, or patrons, who administered their affairs, protected their staffs, and fostered their growth. In the case of royal libraries, these trustees were doubtless nobles of the court. In monastic libraries, the abbot probably appointed a committee of monks to serve as supervisors. The great university libraries of the past were probably administered by a faculty library committee which is still the pattern of university library administration. The library trustee of today is part of a glorious on-going procession which started in the dim early history of civilization and will doubtless continue as long as civilization endures.

How Libraries Began

The history of libraries roughly corresponds to the development of writing materials. Obviously a library of cave paintings or stone carvings would be impracticable, but clay tablets, sheets of papyrus, rolls

MR. GRILL was a trustee of the Lakewood Public Library, Lakewood, Ohio. Statistical revision by the U.S. Office of Education, Division of Library Services and Educational Facilities.

of parchment, and finally books in bindings represent the epochs through which libraries have passed.

During the reign of Sargon I, King of Babylon, who flourished nearly three thousand years before the Christian era, there was a temple library at Nippur containing a vast number of business and commercial records on clay tablets which would seem to suggest that the business library of our day, now a significant feature of library development, had an earlier efflorescence. Assurbanipal, King of Assyria (669–625 B.C.) and conqueror of much of Egypt, established a library of clay tablets in Nineveh, significant today because it is known to have had a librarian, a catalog, and a set of rules and regulations.

From Clay to Papyrus

The transition from clay tablets to papyrus was made in Egypt probably because the plant out of which papyrus is made is native to the Nile region. The first library in Egypt, so far as we now know, was founded by Rameses II about 1275 B.C. Most of its treasures were written on papyrus scrolls. It was housed in a building of typical Egyptian architecture on the front lintel of which was chiseled, "The Dispensary of the Soul," a fitting description which might well be copied on modern libraries.

The Greeks who contributed so much to our Western civilization were the first to establish libraries devoted to the preservation and diffusion of knowledge and they were the precursors of the modern library movement. Many of the early Greek libraries were privately owned, such as that of Aristotle, which at his death he willed to his pupil, Theophrastus, and which was finally taken from Athens to Rome in 98 B.C.

Although the great Alexandrine libraries were located in Egypt, they were founded by Greeks and followed the Greek philosophy of library management and purpose. Two of them were famous and important around 300 B.C., the Serapeum and the Brucheum having about 900,000 rolls of papyrus on their shelves. The Brucheum was destroyed by the Emperor Aurelian in 272 A.D. when he invaded the Nile delta. About 120 years later the Serapeum was destroyed by order of the Emperor Theodosius because he considered it a heathen collection and inimical to Christianity. Bookburning is a sin of very ancient lineage.

Eumenes, King of Pergamum in Asia Minor, had a library of 200,000 rolls which were kept on adjustable shelves supported by wooden brackets. This library marked the beginning of the transition from papyrus to parchment. When Marc Antony overran this small kingdom in the first century B.C., he confiscated the library and presented it to Cleopatra. Possibly these two very famous lovers loved learning in addition to power and romance.

The Libraries of Rome and Arabia

Julius Caesar planned a great library for Rome but in this and in other good intentions he was frustrated by the daggers of Brutus *et al.* However, his successor, the great Augustus, carried out his plans, even amplified them in some respects and libraries began to grow and flourish in the Eternal City. By the time of Hadrian, 125 years later, there were twenty-nine libraries of the Greek type in Rome and about the same number in the rest of the Roman Empire. Pliny, like a modern philanthropist, founded the library in his home town of Comum. As early as 50 A.D. the reading habit had attained such a vogue that books, or parchment rolls, were read by the high elegant caste Romans while they lolled in the famous Roman baths, while they partook of their meals, and were used to induce sleep when they retired for the night. The directors of these Roman libraries were called procurators, the rolls were arranged systematically on shelves and each library had a catalog of the books in its collection. One library of 1,756 rolls was preserved reasonably intact down to modern times by the Vesuvian lava and ashes that fell on Herculaneum.

The great Roman Emperor Constantine started a library in his Eastern capital, Constantinople, about 325 A.D. which in about fifty years accumulated a collection of more than a hundred thousand rolls. After the fall of Rome in 476 and the removal of the court to Constantinople, many royal and monastic libraries were started in eastern Europe. Twenty of the great monastic libraries on Mt. Athos in Greece still survive. They are still great, not so much in the size of their book collections as in the value of their very rare antiquities.

When the Turkish armies conquered Constantinople in 1453, the Greek scholars, who were the librarians in the Roman Empire of the East and the conservators of its culture, fled to the comparative safety of Italy and France carrying many valuable manuscripts and rolls of parchment with them. The thrifty Turks sold many others to book collectors and brokers and these books eventually were purchased for private, public, and monastic libraries in Western Europe and contributed greatly to the advance of the Renaissance which began about this time.

In the wake of the movement which carried the Moslem sword and crescent from Baghdad to Spain came the scholarly Arabs who set up a chain of seventy libraries across southern Europe and north Africa, in addition to reforming mathematical science by introducing the Arabic numeral system to Western civilization. By the tenth century A.D. the great library at Cordova in Spain contained more than six hundred thousand books. It is interesting to note, and an evidence of the catholicity of knowledge, that the works of Aristotle, which influenced all of European science and philosopy for many years, were first translated into the languages of Europe by the Arabs.

The Monastic Phase

After Christianity became well established in Europe the libraries underwent an almost imperceptible change, becoming strong in philosophy and religion and much less concerned with science. Many so called "pagan" manuscripts were destroyed and many more were turned into palimpsests, or manuscripts on which the original pagan writing had been erased and new Christian writing superimposed. Today some of these lost "pagan" works are being recaptured as scholars carefully erase the later writing and with powerful microscopes are able to read the earlier.

The monastic phase of library development began early in the history of Christianity, spread through the Near East and Europe, and in some aspects continues into our own era. All of the significant early Christian libraries were the adjuncts of monasteries. The library of a monastery founded at Caesarea in 309 A.D. eventually grew to more than thirty thousand parchment rolls. The monastic library of St. Macarius in Egypt, founded in 380 A.D., is still in existence, though relatively little used at present. The famous library of Monte Cassino south of Rome lasted and flourished until its destruction by American air power in World War II. It is now being restored, largely with American funds. Other famous monastic libraries were founded at Tours, Cluny, and Clairvaux in France, Fulda in Germany, and St.

Gall in Switzerland. In these may be found the beginnings of some modern library practices. For instance, St. Benedict, among many other rules, set up definite library hours, both for keeping the libraries open and for their compulsory use by the monks. The Augustinian librarians carefully wrote instructions for binding, repairing, cataloging, and shelving their books. The Carthusians were the first to open their great libraries to the public and to lend books to responsible citizens of the community.

As might be expected, the Reformation brought a decline in the importance of monastic libraries, and a corresponding rise in university libraries, many of which came under the proud patronage of nobility and royalty. In France the decline of the monastic library movement was accelerated by the Revolution and these great collections of books were largely distributed among newly founded municipal libraries. A similar development took place in Italy in the years of strife between King and Pope.

The Invention of Printing Revolutionizes Libraries

Probably the greatest impetus the library movement ever received came with the invention of printing from movable type about the middle of the 15th century. As manuscripts and incunabula (books printed from carved wooden blocks, generally prior to 1500 A.D.) were superseded by books printed from movable metallic type, one of the noblest examples of which is the Gutenberg Bible printed at Mayence in Germany about 1456, emperors and kings, noblemen and tycoons began to add to their private libraries. And suddenly books became so cheap that university libraries could afford to add many scholarly, scientific and reference books to their collections. Large and small communities could afford to establish free public libraries and furnish their citizens with books for recreational reading, general culture and vocational information. And probably most important of all, the very possibility of publication stimulated many potential authors to write books which would never have been written in the pre-printing ages.

The rising sun of the Renaissance dissipated the gloom of the Dark Ages and in its dazzling light the founding and fostering of libraries became the principal benevolent projects of some of the outstanding men of the time. The modern era in the development of libraries may be said to have begun about the middle of the 16th Century when the Renaissance was well under way and books began to pour out from printing presses all over Europe.

The Beginning of Public Libraries

At this time public libraries began to take their place along with private and university libraries. The private libraries were mostly of the bibliophile type and reflected the erudition, taste, and hobbies of their owners. The university libraries were largely devoted to scholarship and science and their resources were generally not available to the public. But in the early 1600's public libraries began to appear and to circulate books of general culture, vocational information and recreation among their readers.

Some of the great libraries of antiquity have evolved into famous modern libraries. The great library of the Vatican was founded by Pope Damasus about 375 A.D. He also fostered the revision of the sacred scriptures that has come to be known as the Vulgate Bible. The Vatican library now has more than 700,000 printed books, 7,000 incunabula and 50,000 manuscripts. In 1928 Pope Pius XI began the reorganization of this great library along modern lines, installing modern library methods and techniques and opening it to much wider use.

One of the most famous of the early public libraries is the one founded by Cardinal Mazarin in Paris, which opened in October, 1643 under the direction of the famous librarian, Gabriel Naudé. This library which is still much used by scholars, contains about 250,000 volumes, about 2,000 incunabula, and includes the famous Mazarin Bible, discovered in the library about 1760 and identified as a genuine Gutenberg Bible, the first of several that have since come to light.

Development of National Libraries

The Bibliothéque Nationale, or National Library, overshadows all other libraries in France and ranks as one of the half dozen greatest libraries in the world. It was founded about 1540 by Francis I, first at Fontainbleau, but later moved to Paris where it enjoyed a very rapid growth under Colbert during the reign of Louis XIV. Napoleon enriched it greatly with booty from the libraries of the countries which surrendered to his military might. It now has more than 6,000,000 books, 5,000,000 prints and engravings, 500,000 bound periodicals and 155,000 manuscripts.

Italy has several National Libraries dating back to the national states that occupied the peninsula prior to the unification in recent times. The National Library of Florence was founded in 1714 and contains 4,000,000 volumes and pamphlets, 24,000 manuscripts and 3,600 incunabula or books printed prior to 1500 A.D. Other important Italian libraries are the Laurentian at Florence, the Victor Emmanuel in Rome, the Royal of Naples and the National libraries at Palermo and Turin.

The National Library of Spain at Madrid, now open to the public, contains more than two million volumes and is a rich mine, largely unused under the present regime, of early Spanish and Spanish-American history and accounts of the early voyages that made Spain for a while one of the great world powers.

In Germany at about the time of the Reformation municipal libraries were established in Brunswick, Danzig and Hamburg, and the University libraries at Wittenburg, Halle and Marburg, were among the principal beneficiaries of the breaking up of the monasteries. The Prussian State Library at Berlin is a scholar's library, especially strong in science, art and literature. The largest in Germany, it was started about 1660 by Frederick William, the Great Elector of Brandenburg, largely with confiscated material from the monastic libraries. Frederick the Great who was King of Prussia from 1740 to 1786, friend of Voltaire and admirer of Washington, was one of its greatest benefactors. Prior to World War II it contained nearly three million volumes, 400,000 maps, 55,000 manuscripts and 6,000 incunabula. In 1947 it was combined with the library of the University of Berlin, but the war losses were so great that the new combined institution has less than half the resources of its pre-war predecessor. In all the libraries of Germany, it is estimated that war caused the loss of more than twenty-five million volumes.

As might be expected, all the great cities of Germany had established fine public libraries which prior to World War II ranged in size from 300,000 to 1,000,000 volumes and some of them, Dresden for example, were particularly rich in material relating to the industry or other characteristics which made the city famous. Through union catalogs and interlibrary loans the resources of nearly all the great libraries were available to nearly all German citizens and scholars from all over the world. Some of these libraries are now behind the Iron Curtain and others are recuperating from the vast upheaval of the war.

The National Library of Austria at Vienna was founded in 1440, and prior to World War II contained nearly a million and a half books and many ancient manuscripts written on papyrus. In the old Austro-Hungarian empire there were other fine libraries in Budapest, Cracow, Graz, Lemberg, and Prague with book collections of great value ranging up to two million volumes.

The practical people of Switzerland have fine libraries at Basle, Berne, Zurich, and Geneva with smaller libraries in most of the cantons containing many special technical and scientific collections relating to such industries as watchmaking, hotel keeping and cheese culture.

There are libraries bearing the appellation "Royal" in most of the smaller capital cities of Europe. All of these are now public libraries very widely used, with American library philosophy and ideals beginning to pervade their methods.

Statistics from Russia may properly be labelled as "claims" and probably should be discounted to some extent. The State Public Library of Leningrad, formerly the Russian Imperial Library, claims to have more than six million volumes on its shelves, and the All Union Lenin Memorial Library in Moscow which once was known to have about 3,500,000 volumes, now claims to have 25,000,000 volumes and 2,500,000 manuscripts. There are known to be relatively important libraries in Kiev and other cities and there are claimed to be more than three hundred thousand libraries in all of the Soviet Union. By way of modest comparison, it may be noted that there are 100,320 libraries in the United States, including all public, college and university, special and school libraries.

The earliest libraries in England were in the monasteries. The great university libraries were founded during the monastic period and later profited by the dissolution of some of the church institutions. The Oxford University library was founded in 1327 and during its first century it was so insignificant that the Duke of Gloucester received great praise, a parchment, probably a medal and an honorary degree for donating 130 books from his own library. At about this same time the catalog of the Cambridge University library listed only 122 books. The Oxford library struggled along until about 1600 when Sir Thomas

Bodley became its benefactor and in recognition of his gifts its name was changed to the Bodleian Library. Many of the separate colleges of Oxford and Cambridge have important book collections.

Outranking all other libraries in Great Britain, and one of the truly great libraries of the world, is the British Museum. Founded in 1753, it has accumulated about six million volumes, many by gifts and bequests, and it adds about 60,000 volumes a year to its collection by the operation of the copyright law. It is strong in every department of human knowledge, with manuscripts, books and pamphlets, old and new, on nearly every subject and in nearly every language. One of its many famous borrowers was Karl Marx who wrote most of his monumental *Das Kapital* while sitting at one of the tables in its reading rooms.

Libraries in the United States

The history of libraries in the United States began with the library of Henrico College at Jamestown, Virginia in 1621. This library had a short life as it was destroyed in 1622 when the Indians burned the college building and killed off most of the inhabitants of the town.

The next library and the first permanent one to be founded in the United States started in 1638 when the Rev. John Harvard bequeathed his modest library of 400 books to the little college which had opened its doors in 1636 in Cambridge, Massachusetts. The grateful trustees hurriedly gave his name to the university which now has nearly six million books in its various libraries. In addition to Harvard, other great university libraries were founded at Yale, Princeton, Pennsylvania, Columbia, Brown and Dartmouth during the following century.

The Library of Congress, founded in 1800, is the world's largest establishment devoted to library functions. Its beginnings were very modest. The small book collection was entirely destroyed by the British army in 1814, but the library was re-established the following year when by act of Congress Thomas Jefferson's library of 6,487 volumes was purchased. A devastating fire destroyed more than two thirds of the collection in 1851 and the library languished until 1866 when the scientific books of the Smithsonian Institution were transferred to it. Since 1870 it has acquired a copy of all books copyrighted in the United States and at the present time, with more than fifteen million books and a total collection of approximately sixty million, ranks as one of the largest, if not the largest, and certainly one of the most useful libraries in the world.

The public libraries of America had their beginnings in the club or society libraries such as the one Benjamin Franklin founded in Philadelphia in 1731, which is still active. A number of the older cities of the country, Charleston, South Carolina, for example, still have active membership libraries as well as tax supported public libraries, but most of the private libraries have been merged with public libraries and are open to the general public.

Our First Public Libraries

The tax supported public library movement started about 1833 with Peterboro, New Hampshire, and Burlington, New Jersey, about tied for the honor of being the first in the field. Their greatest development occurred in the last half of the 19th century and the first half of the 20th. In many of the older public libraries, and some of the newer, the tax income is augmented by endowment earnings which often are used for special phases of library work.

The United States is without doubt the leader of the world in the number of library volumes in popular use and in advanced library techniques and administrative methods. Library philosophy in America stresses popular education and service to the public rather than erudition, though the existence of a "Reference Department" in hundreds of public libraries apparently indicates a growing interest in research.

A recent compilation lists 6,922 public libraries in the United States, 2,894 academic libraries, 4,030 special libraries, and 82,641 school libraries; the larger library systems of the country have about 3,833 branch libraries housed in separate buildings, a total of 100,320. There are approximately 683 public libraries in Canada.

No history of the library movement on the North American continent would be complete without mention of the greatest benefactor libraries have ever had. Andrew Carnegie began aiding libraries as early as 1881, since which time more than 2,500 have been started, aided or endowed by Carnegie benefactions. In the early years of this century, so ubiquitous were the typical county seat Carnegie libraries and so standardized their architecture, that one northwest Iowa town attained considerable newspaper publicity by announcing to the world that it did not have a Carnegie library. Up to the present time, the total contributions to libraries by Mr. Carnegie and the various foundations bearing his name are in excess of $73,000,000. A single gift of $5,200,000 in 1901 provided for the construction of approximately forty branch library buildings in New York City.

While Mr. Carnegie was making library history with his wealth, Melvil Dewey was making a very great contribution of a very different nature. He was chief librarian and professor of library economy at Columbia University, later director of the New York State Library and founder and director of the New York State Library School. He, together with R. R. Bowker, was one of the founders of the American Library Association and founder and early editor of *The Library Journal*. However, his greatest contribution to library science and the service for which he will be forever gratefully remembered by all librarians and library users was the invention of the Dewey Decimal Classification system, by which nearly all library books in the United States and Canada and many in Europe are cataloged and shelved and made easily accessible to all users.

On the shelves of all the public libraries in the United States there are more than 330,000,000 volumes and the annual expenditures for library purposes exceed $495,000,000 not counting the cost of new buildings. This is small change, of course, in comparison with our annual expenditures for liquor, tobacco, cosmetics and automobiles.

Of the public library systems in the United States there are eighteen having book collections in excess of a million volumes, the largest being the New York Public Library system with more than nine million books in its main libraries and about eighty branches. The public libraries in such cities as Chicago, Cleveland, Los Angeles, Baltimore, Pittsburgh, Detroit, Cincinnati, Boston, Milwaukee, Newark, Philadelphia, Minneapolis and St. Louis are outstanding, not only because of their size, but also because of the variety and high quality of their services to the people of the communities in which they are located.

These very large library systems differ in degree more than in kind, from the many hundreds of smaller libraries in the United States and Canada. Even the small community library housed in a rented room just off Main Street with a single librarian in charge and with only a few thousand books on the shelves, serves the school children, the young people, the women's clubs, the business interests, the church groups and all the other community agencies in its small way just as a large library with a thousand or more employees does in its large way.

New Chapters in the Library's Long Story
By Virginia G. Young

The latest chapters in the library's long story tell of present-day developments of the concept of accessibility. It was the broadening of accessibility to books which gave America its public libraries, beginning in the latter half of the 19th century.

During the formative years of a widespread public library movement, the ideal was a centrally located free public library with doors open to all. This ideal built libraries in most of the cities and towns of the nation, and at the time represented the peak of accessibility to books and information.

Changing population trends brought about branch libraries, together with mobile library service through bookmobiles reaching far-flung suburbs and rural areas. County libraries, usually part of a regional library system, reach literally millions of persons formerly deprived of library service of any kind.

The concept of the library as an educational institution and information service center has destroyed the former isolation which hampered expansion of library service. Since the first dramatic breakthrough which followed the Library Services Act in 1956, Congress has voted support to many new federal programs in support of public library services and information services. New library construction, expanded library services, augmented and better-trained staffs—all can be obtained with federal assistance. Interlibrary cooperation between all types of libraries—public, school, college, university, and special—further broadened library services available. Particular attention is paid to programs of library service to physically, culturally, and economically disadvantaged citizens.

The very concept of library services itself has changed. New technical processes emerge almost daily for collection and retrieval of information, in which automation plays a leading role. New departments and materials are found essential to the library which formerly housed only books: records, tapes, films, prints, sculpture, Braille, and large-print books—the list grows constantly.

New federal and state programs of library assistance are designed to bring adequate library service to every citizen, with the purpose that every citizen may share alike in opportunities to contribute his talents and abilities.

No, the library's long story has not yet come to its end. New chapters have been written as fresh needs and demands are brought to the library, and new and illustrious chapters are yet to come.

Appendix XI

A Reading List for Library Trustees

Batchelder, Mildred. *Public Library Trustees in the Nineteen Sixties.* ALTA Publication No. 4. Chicago, American Library Trustee Association, 1969.

A review of the literature of trusteeship and, at the same time, an assessment of the role of the trustee in library development.

The Bowker Annual of Library and Book Trade Information. New York, R. R. Bowker Company.

A one-volume reference shelf of activities, organizations, and statistics published annually.

Connally, John. "The Governor's Conference on Libraries; Birthplace for Citizen Action." *State Government.* (Summer 1967), 158–64.

The Governor of Texas describes the purposes, patterns, and results of such conferences, drawing first hand from a very successful one in Texas.

Corrigan, Dorothy D. *Workbook for a Successful Workshop.* ALTA Publication No. 1. Chicago, American Library Trustee Association, 1967.

Step-by-step discussion of elementary principles for planning, presenting, and evaluating a workshop prepared especially for trustee groups, but useful to any group.

———— and Hoyt R. Galvin. "Library Building Consulting: Problems and Ethics." *ALA Bulletin* (May 1968), 505–10.

Currier, Lura G., compiler. *Contracts and Agreements for Public Library Service.* Public Library Reporter No. 6. Chicago, American Library Association, 1958.

Collection of contracts and excerpts of contracts in use by library systems.

Frantz, John C. "The Small Public Library—Its Establishment, Organization and Development." No. 2 of the Series: *The Small Public Library.* Chicago, American Library Association, 1962.

228

Garceau, Oliver. *Public Library in the Political Process.* New York, Columbia University Press, 1949.

The volume in the Public Library Inquiry devoting special attention to the library board in its relation both to the library and to the governing authority. Based on detailed study of boards established under differing conditions. Provocative and outspoken.

Gorham, William, Elizabeth Drew, and Aaron Wildavsky. "PPBS: Its Scope and Limits." *The Public Interest,* No. 8 (Summer 1967), 3–48.

An article explaining planning, programming, and budgeting system.

Holden, Barbara B. *The State Trustee Organization,* ALTA Publication No. 2. Chicago, American Library Trustee Association, 1968.

Practical discussion of methods to organize, revitalize, or strengthen statewide association of library trustees.

Leigh, Robert D. *Public Library in the United States.* New York, Columbia University Press, 1950.

A broad discussion of the many factors influencing public library service in the United States, summarizing the findings of the Public Library Inquiry.

Library Building Institute. *Libraries, Building for the Future.* Ed. by Robert J. Shaw. Chicago, American Library Association, 1967.

Proceedings of the Library Building Institute and ALTA Workshop in 1965 which includes an examination of the trustee's role in planning and building.

Lynch, Mrs. Weldon. *Guidelines for Holding a Governor's Conference on Libraries.* ALTA Publication No. 3. Chicago, American Library Trustee Association, 1968.

How to organize for, plan, and run a conference, including committee structure and responsibilities, and a calendar of deadlines.

Maurois, André. *Public Libraries and Their Mission.* UNESCO, 1961.

A splendid pamphlet on public library purposes.

National Library Week. *Organization Handbook.* New York, National Library Week, 1967.

Phinney, Eleanor. *Library Adult Education in Action.* Chicago, American Library Association, 1956.

A series of case reports on "What is happening in five different libraries with well-developed educational services for adults." Includes excellent helps to studying a community.

Public Library Association. *Interlibrary Cooperation: A Sampling of Interlibrary Cooperation.* Public Library Reporter No. 12. Chicago, American Library Association, 1967.

Directors of five on-going interlibrary projects describe them.

Reach Out With Books: Proceedings of the Workshop for Library Trustees. Chicago, American Library Trustee Association, 1966.

Proceedings of a one-day meeting in New York which considers the ways in which books can be used to reach all segments of the community.

Sinclair, Dorothy. *Administration of the Small Public Library.* Chicago, American Library Association, 1965.

Realistic, practical guidelines and principles for making wise policy decision and solving everyday problems.

The Small Public Library: A series of guides for community librarians and trustees. Chicago, American Library Association, 1962–63.

These pamphlets, developed under the Small Libraries Project, are all of value to trustees.

Smith, Hannis S. "Cooperative Approach to Library Service." No. 16 of the series: *The Small Public Library.* Chicago, American Library Association, 1962.

Standards for library service adopted by the American Library Association. All are available from the Publishing Department, American Library Association, Chicago.

Interim Standards for Small Public Libraries: Guidelines Toward Achieving the Goals of Public Library Service. American Library Association, 1962.

Minimum Standards for Public Library Systems, 1966. ALA Public Library Association, 1966.

Standards for Children's Services in Public Libraries. ALA Public Library Association, 1964.

Standards for College Libraries. ALA Association of College and Research Libraries, 1959. (Reprints from *College and Research Libraries,* 20: 274–80 [July 1959].)

Standards for Junior College Libraries. ALA Association of College and Research Libraries, 1960. (Reprinted from *College and Research Libraries,* 21: 200–26 [May 1960].)

Standards for Library Functions at the State Level. ALA American Association of State Libraries, 1963.

Standards for Library Services for the Blind and Visually Handicapped. ALA Library Administration Division, 1967.

Standards of Quality for Bookmobile Service. ALA Public Library Association, 1963.

Standards for School Media Programs. ALA American Association of School Librarians and NEA Dept. of Audiovisual Instruction, 1969.

Young Adult Services in the Public Library. ALA Public Library Association, 1960.

"Suggested Policies for Public Libraries." No. 2A of the series: *The Small Public Library.* Chicago, American Library Association, 1963.

Wallace, Sarah Leslie, editor. *Friends of the Library: Organization and Activities.* American Library Association, 1962.

Twelve articles concerning citizen support of public, county, state, and college and university libraries.

Warncke, Ruth. "Planning Good Library Meetings." *School Libraries,* 11:15–20 (January 1962).

Wessells, Helen. "The Public Library: A Tool for Modern Living." No. 1 of the series: *The Small Public Library.* Chicago, American Library Association, 1962.

Wheeler, Joseph L. "The Small Library Building." No. 13 of the series: *The Small Public Library.* Chicago, American Library Association, 1962.

———— and Herbert Goldhor. *Practical Administration of Public Libraries.* New York, Harper & Row, 1962.

" . . . a guide to management principles and their practical application in public libraries." Extensive bibliographies.

White, Ruth M., editor. *Public Library Policies—General and Specific.* Public Library Reporter No. 9. Chicago, American Library Association, 1960.

Selected policy statements in actual use by 200 public libraries of various sizes which provide a useful guide for libraries and trustees formulating policy statements.

Winser, Marian Manley. *A Handbook for Library Trustees.* New York, R. R. Bowker Company, 1959.

Young, Virginia G., "The Trustee of a Small Public Library." No. 3 of the series: *The Small Public Library.* Chicago, American Library Association, 1962.

Index